Coach Chris Fore is one of the best in the business at pas[sing] knowledge to his coaching brethren. In putting this book [together], [Fore scoured the] country for valuable input from over 100 state champion football coaches. He does a masterful job of blending high-level coaching concepts and time-tested football strategies into an easy-to-follow, digestible format that football coaches from all levels will be able to apply to their own programs. This book is fully loaded with championship ideas that will help your team win more than games.

Mike Podoll
Associate Publisher/Editor
This Is AFCA Magazine and FootballCoachDaily.com

This book is well researched and is a must-have for every coach's library. All coaches, regardless of their experience, can gain from its contents. *Building Championship-Caliber Football Programs: Inside the Locker Rooms and Minds of State Champion Head Football Coaches* gives the reader the insight to establish a championship team at any level of football.

Dan Dodd
Athletic Director and Head Football Coach
Capistrano Valley Christian School

Chris Fore took an ingenious idea and executed it well—just like you'd expect from a football coach. Taking people inside the locker rooms and the minds of the most successful high school football coaches in the nation is fascinating. Relating the information from the viewpoint of a coach makes *Building Championship-Caliber Football Programs: Inside the Locker Rooms and Minds of State Champion Head Football Coaches* informative and entertaining. I absolutely loved so many parts of this book and I recommend it for every coach and aspiring coach.

Kevin Acee
Columnist, TV Host, and Former San Diego Chargers Beat Writer
San Diego Union-Tribune

In a day and age when the pressure is higher than it's ever been for high school football coaches, it's refreshing to see that many coaches continue to have a passion for football and instructing young student-athletes, and are willing to share what makes them tick, what brings success to their football programs, and how they motivate their players. I've known Chris for over 15 years and his passion for coaching and helping coaches become better, not just as football coaches, but as leaders of today's youth, is evident in this collection of a wide range of approaches from coaches across the country.

Brandon Huffman
National Recruiting Analyst
Fox Sports

Chris Fore's *Building Championship-Caliber Football Programs: Inside the Locker Rooms and Minds of State Champion Head Football Coaches* should be on the bookshelf of every person interested in high school football. It is for coaches, parents, and fans at all levels. The content makes this book an instant classic—it is insightful, poignant, humorous, and thought-provoking, as well as a map to success that transcends sport.

Harry Welch
Head Football Coach
Santa Margarita Catholic High School (CA)

Having covered high school sports in Southern California for more than 35 years, I know how difficult it is to come up with new ideas for stories. That's why it is exciting to see a new idea come to fruition—a book discussing leadership lessons for building championship-caliber football programs compiled by simply asking coaches who guided their teams to state championships in 2011 for their secrets to success. It's an excellent way to compare, contrast, evaluate, and take or leave suggestions, values, understandings, misconceptions, and anything else from men who have proven they can lead players and teenagers in a very difficult venue. Hearing from a variety of coaches from many different areas of the country provides invaluable information for anyone who loves high school football and admires how leadership is executed.

Eric Sondheimer
Columnist
Los Angeles Times

Student-athletics is heralded as teaching important life lessons such as teamwork, perseverance, and determination. For many in our society, sport serves a higher purpose than simple entertainment. Chris's book draws on the collective wisdom of over 100 coaches from successful high school football programs. His painstaking effort to illuminate what separates the champion from the also-ran comes through with great clarity. This book is a penetrating look into various coaching and leadership perspectives. The voices of the coaches come through loud and clear, providing valuable leadership nuggets and lessons for any coach.

Cory Dobbs, Ed.D.
Founder and President
The Academy for Sport Leadership

Chris Fore has hit a home run with his book *Building Championship-Caliber Football Programs: Inside the Locker Rooms and Minds of State Champion Head Football Coaches*. He has done an extensive study of state championship teams and the men who built them. I appreciate his desire to share this vast amount of wisdom with us. If you coach football, or any sport, this book is an invaluable resource. The insight into creating a championship team is a good read for the veteran and rookie coach alike. I enjoyed this book—once I began reading it I had to finish. I appreciate both the author and the coaches who were willing to discuss their outstanding knowledge of championship football. Thank you, Coach Fore, for the hundreds of hours of research you have put into this book. More importantly, thanks for sharing it with us!

Gregory Ireland
Former Head Football Coach
Murrieta (CA) Valley High School

Building Championship-Caliber Football Programs: Inside the Locker Rooms and Minds of State Champion Head Football Coaches doesn't necessarily deal with winning games or even state championships but rather with building long-term successful programs and developing student-athletes on and off the field. Chris Fore utilizes not only the responses of 108 coaches who won state championships in 2011 but also his own experience as a coach, which includes a trip to the Southern California section semifinals and a league championship, and his years as a player on a team with championship coaches. As Fore's first chapter notes, the true mission of a coach isn't necessarily to win, but rather to build and develop. Fore's research and personal experience will provide excellent guidance for coaches to improve their programs and their players.

Because Fore wrote this book prior to the 2012 high school football season, it doesn't discuss how he applied the knowledge gained from his research to help Excelsior Charter School win the Southern Section eight-man championship and the mythical eight-man state championship as the Eagles' athletic director and special teams coordinator. His role in Excelsior's championship is perhaps the best illustration of how applying the content of his book can make a football program successful.

Joe Naiman
Freelance Sportswriter

Building Championship-Caliber Football Programs

Inside the Locker Rooms and Minds of State Champion Head Football Coaches

Chris Fore

JESSE & JULES,
GOOD LUCK
BUILDING
CHAMPIONS
WHERE YOU ARE.

COACHES
CHOICE™

ISBN: 978-1-60679-288-9
Library of Congress Control Number: 2013956462
Book layout: Cheery Sugabo
Cover design: Cheery Sugabo
Front cover photo: Mim Stokes Brown, St. George's High School (TN)
Front cover background graphic: Stockphoto/Thinkstock

Coaches Choice
P.O. Box 1828
Monterey, CA 93942
www.coacheschoice.com

Dedication

I dedicate this book to my high school coach, Tom Pack.

I grew up in a rural North San Diego County town called Fallbrook. I was lucky enough to grow up in one of the heydays of Fallbrook Warrior football: the 1980s.

Coach Pack began coaching the Warrior football team in 1971 as an assistant and later became the head football coach, a post he held until one year after I graduated in 1994. He was the athletic director for 23 years. As a junior and senior, I was able to be his teacher's assistant one class period a day. This experience with Coach Pack inspired me to become a head football coach and an athletic director. My love affair with coaching started as a senior in high school, when I was able to coach his freshmen team after a car accident ended my playing career. I will be forever grateful for that opportunity.

Many boys became men under the guidance of Coach Pack. I am only one of hundreds. Coach, you did a dynamite job of building a championship-caliber football program at Fallbrook High School. You built a program that we all looked forward to playing in—one that we mimicked on the fields of La Paloma and Potter Junior High. We argued during recess about who was Billy Dunckel, Ty Barksdale, Scott Barrick, or Jamie Miramontes. And for goodness sakes, we always wanted to "Beat Vista" on those playgrounds.

Coach Pack, thank you for your influence in my life and career.

Acknowledgments

This is the first book I've written, and I can tell you one of the most important things I have learned through this process: you cannot put together a book of this nature by yourself. I would like to acknowledge several people who have helped me put this book together.

My amazing bride, Christine—Lovey, thank you so much for supporting me every single step of the way with this project. From the very first time I told you about it on the couch, and you telling me to go for it, to the many days I left you alone with our three kids so I could do research at the library in Redondo, to going to bed by yourself so I could work late on it in Victorville. You could not have been more supportive. Thank you, I love you!

Dr. James Peterson and Coaches Choice—You sold me the perfect book for a first-year head football coach at a clinic in 2003; it was Competitive Leadership by Brian Billick. Thank you for starting my love of reading books for coaches by coaches. You are the best in the business, and I am both humbled and thankful that you would publish this book. Thank you!

The 2011 state championship head football coaches—Easily put, this book simply doesn't exist without your cooperation and tremendous feedback. I really appreciate you allowing not only me, but coaches for generations, to step inside your program to learn from you. So many of you were so humble about your success. I appreciated that. I have learned countless lessons from you all. Thank you!

Perry Krosschell, Bear Schoolmeester, Jeff Hauge, C.J. Del Balso, Steve Chamberlin, Matt Cobb—These five men represent all of the coaches I've coached alongside over the years. These five specifically have been like brothers to me, and have taught me so much about the game both between and outside of the lines. The philosophies I speak about in this book were shaped by you as much as anyone. I have appreciated each and every coach along the way; there are more than 30 of them. Thank you!

My Family—You have been supporting my coaching endeavors in many different ways since 1993. Thank you for always being there. From bringing snacks for after the game to running the snack bar to phone calls and Facebook® messages, your support and encouragement has been a source of inspiration to always do my best.

Jeff Dubransky—Thank you for the encouragement and editing when this book was in the infancy stages. You have no idea how much you inspired me to follow through with this idea in the early months. Thank you, Duby, for that, and for helping me with editing. Thank you!

Tim Riter and Karen Bale—You two are phenomenal authors who have inspired me along the way with words and emails of encouragement and advice. I would have been totally lost without your help as published authors. Thank you!

Jack and Laura Hamilton—When money was very tight, you stepped in to buy the laptop I wrote this book on. Thank you for believing in me and this project enough to do that. I would not have been able to complete this without your financial assistance. Thank you!

Nate, Taylor, and Josiah—This book would have been a lot easier if you three kiddos were not around. But I would not change that for the ability to write a thousand books. One day, your mom will tell you how annoying this book project was to her because there were many days and nights I was not around to help. I love each of you so much, and hope that one day you will be able to use life lessons from this book to help yourself and others.

Contents

Dedication 7

Acknowledgments 8

Introduction 12

Chapter 1: It's Not About Winning:
Oxymoron of the Highest Sort 17

Chapter 2: Stay the Course: Developing Your Philosophy 25

Chapter 3: Coaching the Heart of the Athlete 33

Chapter 4: The Little Things: Daily Discipline
With the Fundamentals 43

Chapter 5: Developing a Work Ethic:
Teaching Your Team to Put in the Time 53

Chapter 6: Leadership: Creating Influence and Direction 63

Chapter 7: Team Chemistry: The Most
Overlooked Key to Success 73

Chapter 8: Mental Toughness: Getting the Mind Right 83

Chapter 9: Preparation: Leave No Stone Unturned 93

Chapter 10: Building Trust and Confidence 105

Appendix: Survey Responses From Contributing
State Champion Head Football Coaches 113

About the Author 225

Introduction

After the 2011 high school football season I set out to learn from the "best of the best"—state champion football coaches from all over the nation—in order to become a better football coach myself. In 2012, our team won its first state championship in history!

Learning From the Best of the Best

The 2011 football season was one of the most depressing seasons of my life. The 2011 football season was one of the most relaxing seasons of my life. The 2011 football season was one of the best of my life. Isn't that something?

It was the most depressing season of my life because it was the first season in the previous 11 years that I wasn't on the field coaching. The first season I didn't have working with amazing coaches and the players who make this job so rewarding. That was the depressing part. Not having a game plan to work toward each week. Not being able to experience the thrill of victory and the agony of defeat with my brotherhood. A new superintendent hired at the private school where I was the athletic director and head football coach wanted to bring in his own guy. So after winning a league championship in November 2010, four months later I was looking for a job.

However, it was one of the most relaxing seasons of my life because I didn't have that constant pressure that comes with being a head coach. To be honest, it was kind of nice getting a break from the high time demands and the physical, mental, psychological, and emotional strain that comes from a long season of 70-hour weeks as a head football coach. After eight straight years of being a head coach, a job that really doesn't have an "off-season," it was a good break to get away from the fundraising, the Booster Club meetings, the parents, the grade checks, the officials, and all of those things that aren't the fun and glamorous parts of the job.

It was one of the best seasons of my life because I got to go to any game I wanted to. That was a lot of fun. When you are in the heat of your own season, you don't get to just pick and choose what football teams to go watch. You have to coach, and if you have a free Friday or Saturday night because of a bye, you have to get out and scout a future opponent. There were a few times over the last 10 years I got to choose a game to go to, but not more than three.

I do remember going to watch Reggie Bush two times when he was in high school. As a junior, I saw him play at my old high school, Fallbrook High. And as a senior, I saw him throw a 95-yard halfback pass for a touchdown versus Oceanside! It was an amazing play, and happened right in front of me. I was standing behind the end zone. My stepfather saw him play as a sophomore and called me to say, "This kid is going to the NFL." He has watched a lot of high school football and never made such a declaration. I started reading about him, and knew that I wanted to see him in action. Fortunately, I was able to do that. Can you imagine having both NFL quarterback Alex Smith and NFL running back Reggie Bush both on your high school roster?

That was the good thing about not coaching in 2011; I was able to go to any game I wanted to. I actually worked as a reporter for part of the season for an online outfit called Patch.com. They asked me to do a special feature on a new head coach in town at a school named Saddleback Valley Christian. So I went out to their practice and interviewed this new coach, Justin Reber. It was very interesting being on the other side of the coin. As I got to know him and learn about his philosophies, I got to thinking, "This would be awesome to do all over the country." To be able to speak to coaches about how they run their programs, dissect their brains about the hows and whys and whats regarding their philosophies. That was the first time I thought about putting this book together, on my drive home after hanging out at the Warriors practice, and talking with Coach Reber. I watched about 35 high school football games in 2011; about 25 in person and 10 on the television.

In January 2012, I saw a list of the state champions on MaxPreps.com. That is when a light bulb went on in my head. "What if I contacted all of these coaches about their philosophies and methods?" I asked myself while thinking back to my afternoon with Coach Reber. I knew I couldn't do this in person, as great as that would be. But the next day, I started to find these coaches by email. I started emailing them one by one. Following is the email I sent to the state championship football coaches all over our nation.

Dear Coach,

Congratulations on your state championship! I'm sure that you are very proud of your boys and your entire staff.

I've coached football for 12 years. I started as a frosh offensive line coach at my alma mater (Fallbrook High School in the San Diego Section, California), and have been in the private sector for the last 10 years, where I've been the head football coach at two private schools here in Southern California (Linfield School and Capistrano Valley Christian).

I absolutely love studying, reading, and learning from the best of the best. I love to read autobiographies of great football coaches, to pick from their brains, and apply a few nuggets to my program.

I've been thinking about doing a project regarding coaching for a long time, and I'm finally pulling trigger. Here is where you come in. I'm reaching out to all of the head coaches from the state champion football in the nation. I'm asking just a few questions in an attempt to learn about what made their programs so successful this past season.

I will take the quotes and answers that you give me and put them all together in a book format to further our profession, to help develop coaches, and most importantly, learn for myself. The title will most likely be *How We Won*.*

I will share the success of *your* program and *your leadership* with football coaches all over the world. Would you be willing to answer just a few questions for me? I will use your answers unedited; cite you and your school as the source.

Simply return your response to me via email at statechampsbook@gmail.com. The three questions I have for you are:
1. What did you do differently this year from the other programs in your league, your section, your state that enabled your success as a state champion?
2. What piece of advice would you give to a head coach who wants to win a state championship?
3. What do you consider the one most important aspect of your championship team this year? How did you develop that in your program?

Thank you so much, Coach, I know your time is valuable.
Chris Fore, CAA
MA Athletic Administration and Coaching

There were 366 state champions from our 50 states in 2011. Every state manages their championship format differently. For instance, California only recognizes five state champions; their Open Division is open to any school in the state regardless of enrollment. Then, they have four other divisions based on enrollment. California has a population of about 38 million people. Massachusetts, on the other hand, with less than 7 million people, recognizes 21 state champions. Some states like Texas break up their championship format into private and public schools. So, you might have six divisions of private school state champions, and 12 divisions of public school state champions.

Out of these 366 state champions, I was able to find contact information for the head football coach, athletic director, or principal for all but 24 schools. If you were a 2011 state champion and are not featured in this book, it is because I never heard back from you. I sent emails or made phone calls to every school between four to six times between January and April of 2012. I did receive responses from the head coaches at 108 schools from 42 different states.

*Note: The title was later changed to *Building Championship-Caliber Football Programs: Inside the Locker Rooms and Minds of State Champion Head Football Coaches*.

The hardest part about this entire process was tracking down these coaches. I literally had to search for the school online, then I searched for the football program on the school's website, and then I searched for the football coaches' email. Sometimes, I would find their email on the staff directory. This process of simply collecting emails took quite a while. I collected responses from coaches for three months before deciding that I had received enough of a response to move forward with a book. The responses were fascinating to me, and as I shared them via my own Facebook and Twitter® accounts, I knew right away that this book idea would be a hit. Other coaches really liked reading what their peers were telling me in their responses.

One coach from South Carolina told me the following:

> "Find out what others are doing that are winning in your area, see if you can use some of that in your program, and continue to build. Continue to learn from others. Getting the kids to buy into your system."
>
> —Chris Miller, Byrnes High School (SC)

I was excited to see many coaches respond with quotes like this, suggesting that doing research and looking around at other programs was a key for them in putting together a competitive football program. Coaches were very supportive of this book idea, and ready to jump on board. That really got me excited for this project. What Coach Miller says is what is at the heart of this book: finding out what others successful coaches are doing, and seeing what you can use to build your program. I've always believed in being a lifelong learner. As a football coach, it is so important to continue to learn and grow in this profession.

What I learned from this research is in the pages that follow. I have broken down this extensive research from these 108 state champion head football coaches into 10 chapters. These are 10 main leadership lessons to build your football program, given to you by some of the best high school coaches in the nation. I've used their philosophies and quotes as the framework for this book.

1

It's Not About Winning:
Oxymoron of the Highest Sort

Nichol DelPercio, Middletown (DE) High School

"A life of frustration is inevitable for any coach whose main enjoyment is winning."

—Former NFL head coach Chuck Noll

It is interesting to have a chapter in a book about building a championship-caliber football program that is entitled "It's Not About Winning." It is like reading a book about riding a bike telling you that it is not about pedaling. However, one of the most common statements I received back from the 2011 state champion head coaches is "It is not about winning." Coach after coach made statements to me like "If you want to win a state championship, do not think about winning a state championship" or "Do not focus on winning," or "Winning is simply an afterthought."

At first, it was hard for me to decipher if these coaches really meant this, or if it was just easy for them to say since they had just won a state championship. Many of the coaches surveyed have won multiple state championships, and have career winning percentages that are heavily lopsided toward the winning side. Isn't it easy for them to say "Don't worry about winning?" How many 0-10 coaches say "Do not worry about winning?"

But when you read through all of the research, they really mean this. Winning can't be one of the sole focuses of your program and your purpose as a coach. If it is, and you don't win, you will have a very, very long season. Trust me, I know.

In 2008, I had my first (and I hope to God, my last) winless season. We went 0-10. It was horrible. It was a perfect storm of aggressive scheduling in fall of 2006, my first year at this particular school, combined with an enrollment that was dwindling as a function of the U.S. financial collapse. I went from having 30 kids in the program to about 18 in just two years. Our numbers in the football program matched the numbers, percentage-wise, of kids we lost in the school. It is tough to build a winning program with this few varsity football players. And I have always loved scheduling up on the competition food chain. Eight teams we lost to that year made the CIF playoffs, and a few played for the championship; one was the state champion in California, who also just happened to be the champion of our very own league. Our schedule was brutal.

Suffice to say that each week got more and more frustrating. As the losses mounted, we pressed—I pressed—for a win. I totally lost focus that year. It wasn't about the technique, the play calling, the preparation; it was all about getting a win. Getting the proverbial monkey off our back. I am embarrassed to say I failed my team, my coaching staff, and my school that year as I put winning ahead of everything else. I lost focus on my purpose as a football coach, and why I got in this business to start with.

Your Purpose as a Coach

"The advice I would give a coach is not to be coaching football to become a champion. Your job as a coach is to teach your athletes

how to become better people in society. If you are coaching to win, you are in it for the wrong reasons."

—Mike Rowe, Rocori High School (MN)

"Do not coach just to win a state championship. Coach for the right reasons, such as loving the game, being a part of a team, being a positive influence on young people, using the platform of football to affect the community, etc. I have won five state championships, and I can tell you that it can feel very empty if that is all that you are coaching for."

—Tim Goodwin, Marion Local High School (OH)

It is time to dig deep. A gut check. Halftime in your coaching career, so to speak. You know that time when you go in to the locker room to circle up with your coaches, to look back on the first half of the game in order to evaluate what has happened? This moment is that time for you. Why do you coach? For what reasons are you in this profession? I know it is not about the money.

Have you ever made a list of why you coach? Have you ever written a mission statement for yourself as a coach, to help guide you?

I love what Coach Rowe says at the beginning of this section about coaching for the wrong reasons. Is there any type of wrong motivation for you personally? That year I referred to, when I was 0-10, I failed to remember the reasons I started coaching. All that became important to me was winning a stinking game. I lost sight of what Coach Rowe refers to as why we coach: to teach our kids to become better people in society. I had ample opportunities that season to teach my players. Unfortunately, I taught them the wrong things that winless season. Like Coach Goodwin says, if your focus is not right, your coaching will feel very empty. At the end of that season, I did feel empty. It felt like a wasted season as I evaluated my purpose that season.

Most of you probably got in to this profession because of the reasons I did. You love football, you love working with teenagers, you love teaching, you had a great high school football experiences with great coaches who you admired. So, at a young age, probably during high school or right afterward, you made a decision that you wanted to get in to coaching because you wanted to be like those men who devoted so much of their time to shaping you as a person. Does that have anything to do with winning? Absolutely not.

You probably started coaching for peanuts, or maybe just a free hat, t-shirt, and jacket. You wanted to be a part of a coaching staff and football program so bad that you made decisions to sacrifice financially, to miss things your friends were doing during the summer, and maybe you even to take a job at a less desirable school. But you did it to coach. Do not lose sight of that. Remember, the reasons you wanted to coach probably do not have much at all to do about winning. These state championship coaches testify to the fact that if you grind and grind it out just to win, you will be empty if that doesn't happen, and you will be empty if it does happen.

Before you put this book down today, I want you to write out a few of your purposes for coaching. This step will help guide you. Why do you coach? Why do you *truly* coach? The Time-Out section at the end of this chapter will help you with this exercise, and help you have a laser focus about your purpose as a coach. My personal list follows:

Why I Coach

- A burning passion to do so.
- I enjoy working with people, specifically teenagers.
- I love the game of football.
- To embrace the challenge.
- To use my gifts/talents of leadership and administration.

What Motivates You?

Now that you've thought through why you coach, I want you to take a look at what motivates you to coach. Obviously, that has a lot to do with why you coach. But do not get the two confused. I love my wife because she is an amazing person and I have made a commitment to love her. Those are two reasons *why* I love her. What *motivates* me to love her is different. What motivates me to love her is a daily relationship that goes two ways. I am motivated to love her by what she does for our family, by what she does for me, by how I see her react to my love. It is different.

What motivates you to coach? Just like my motivation for loving my wife will change on a day-to-day and year-to-year basis, I strongly believe that our motivation to coach will change from year to year *if* we aren't focused solely on the winning aspect. The reason this motivation will change is because our surroundings and our team culture changes every year.

> *"Not to focus on winning a state championship. If it's meant to be, it will happen. Focus on developing your student athletes in all areas to prepare them to be successful in life."*
>
> —Mike Boyd, Nouvel Catholic Central High School (MI)

Coach Boyd says that we need to be coaching and teaching to help prepare our kids to be successful in life. "Successful" is going to look different from community to community. In some communities, it is a huge success just to graduate from your high school, while in others that result is just expected. The success in that community might be a college degree.

In a Christian community, the "success" of your kids will be determined by how close to Christ they have become as a result of being in your program. This drive should be what motivates you.

> "If your goal is to win a state championship, change your goal. If your passion is to build young men of character, faith, and a strong work ethic, build men who will be great fathers, husbands, and sons. Build relationships that change lives.
>
> "The state championships become the outcome of building what really matters. Putting first things first; placing Christ as the most important thing in your program. The closeness of the players and coaches. The seniors had a lot to do with that; they made it about the whole team. There was no selfishness on this team.
>
> "Maybe the biggest reason was: at Midland Christian, we have won five state championships since 2000, but we were four years from our last one. The drought was hard, and it helped this group to develop an attitude of 'Whatever you say, Coach, we will do. You have four rings; we have none. No questions asked. We will do whatever you say.'"
>
> —Greg McClendon, Midland (TX) Christian High School

> "We believe that you develop the whole athlete with the mind-set of becoming a champion in every area of life. We ask our players to live like a champion.
>
> "We believe that you become a champion first, and then you win championships. Winning a championship doesn't make you a champion in our eyes. Doing things right all the time will make it habit-forming. It is easy to do it right on game night if you are in the habit of doing it all the time: practice effort, academics, citizenship, character, community service, etc."
>
> —Kirk Fridrich, Union High School (OK)

For Coach Fridrich, the motivation for him is getting his kids in the "habit of doing the right thing all the time: practice effort, academics, citizenship, character, community service, etc." This motivation will serve his coaching staff well in a 0-10 season or a 10-0 season. This motivation should serve as a road map for his staff. His staff should come back to this motivation throughout the course of the year.

I coached against a man named Noel Johnson for several years, and then recruited him to come coach on my staff when he semi-retired from the game. He is a great person, with great Christian ethics, and since I was at a Christian school at the time, I wanted him to coordinate my defense. He was excellent at continually reminding our coaching staff of our motivation. That was during a year when we did not lose a league game. He would constantly bring up that we were doing great things besides just winning. This was good for me to see, and it was wonderful for some of the younger coaches on our staff to see. Our purpose was not just to win a league championship, but to teach kids about Christian character. Coach Johnson looked past our immediate success because he was motivated by teaching values and ethics to his players.

> *"It rarely has to do with what we did this year but rather what habits did we establish three to four years ago, when these current seniors where in their freshman and sophomore years, that paid huge dividends this season. Truthfully, I'm not sure what other folks do, but we have a system and structure in place that allows us to help our athletes grow as people, students, and athletes. We purposefully teach a character curriculum, and we think that part of our success is the character development we do with our players throughout the year. We work awfully hard in the weight room, on the practice field, and in the film room, too."*

—Frederick Bouchard, Staley High School (MO)

Enjoy the Process

> *"Be yourself. Do not focus on winning a state championship. Focus on daily excellence."*

– Harry Welch, Santa Margarita Catholic High School (CA)

Coach Welch is a record-setter in California. He has won three state championships with three different schools in three different divisions—and he did all of this in just six years. California started crowning state champions in 2006 after a long hiatus with not having an "official process" or champion. He won a Division 1 state championship (when they had three divisions) with Canyon High School when they knocked off Concord De La Salle in 2006. Then, after more than two decades at Canyon, he went to a little school of 400 kids in San Juan Capistrano called St. Margaret's Episcopal School. He won 42 games in a row with them, and won a Small Schools State Championship in 2008. Then, he went to Santa Margarita High School in 2011 and won a state championship there in the second largest division (when they had four divisions). He has won a total of nine CIF Section Championships—five with Canyon, three with St. Margaret's, and one with Santa Margarita.

As I have gotten to know this California legend since we competed against each other in the Academy League while he was at St. Margaret's, what I appreciate the most about Coach Welch is that he truly appreciates the daily preparation of his troops more than any coach I know. For him, it really is about making his team better each and every day. As he says, "Be yourself." His teams play with more discipline than any team I have ever seen, at any level of football; most coaches who have competed against him will agree with me on this.

I have asked Coach Welch over several lunch conversations how he gets his kids to win. And he always reminds me that it is not about winning. It is about the process, the road you are on toward Friday night. He truly enjoys that process. It is what motivates him, and why he coaches. He says that if the kids are disciplined on the field, they will be disciplined off the field, in the classroom, in their jobs, in their marriages, etc. His focus in demanding them to become great players is so that they will become great people. The two go hand in hand.

Coach Lorenzano also understands this focus on the daily preparation as your focal point and motivation:

> *"We never worry about winning championships. We only concern ourselves with three things: What is our attitude? What is our effort? Did we get better each week?"*
>
> —Vincent Lorenzano, Bishop Chatard High School (IN)

> *"My advice would be to coach one week at a time, and don't make it about a championship. When teams work to get better each and every day, championships take care of themselves. Championships are a result of bringing a group of kids together, motivating them, and getting them to believe in each other and what your coaches are selling. Coaches' jobs are to teach, motivate, and try to get a group of kids to become the best team that they can be. Our coaches are great teachers and are men of faith. I believe [these men are] great role models … Their walk of faith keeps life in perspective … God has blessed us."*
>
> —Andy Lowry, Columbine High School (CO)

"I'll Have Another Team Next Year."

I will never forget my freshman football coach at Fallbrook High School, Scott Carpenter saying this time after time. He usually said it out of frustration when we weren't doing our best. He was indicating that we were wasting his time on the field by our lack of effort and attention to detail to get better that practice. I would get offended at this statement. It ticked me off. "Hey," I thought, "This is *this* year. Who cares about next year, Coach?"

Now, I understand it. He would say, "I'll have another 20 freshmen football teams, you'll only have one." He was sending a message to us to make the most out of our frosh year of football. Don't take it for granted. He wasn't writing us off; he was motivating us in a certain way.

Looking at this statement through a different lens though, as a coach, you won't ever have *this* team again. You will never have this group of boys to motivate, teach, encourage, inspire, etc. We need to make the most out of every opportunity with the team we have in teaching them about character and life lessons. Remember, it is not about winning. It is about more than that. You will only have *this* team one time. You will have another team next year. Do not blow it by putting winning as your main priority. It is not worth it.

Time-Out

1. How and why did you start coaching?
2. Why are you still coaching?
3. What do you enjoy the most about coaching?
4. List two players for whom you have had a major influence in their lives, and try to identify why you had that impact on them.
5. Take the information from questions 1 through 4, and write two to three sentences that will serve as your personal mission statement as a coach.

2

Stay the Course:
Develop Your Philosophy

Nichol DelPercio, Middletown (DE) High School

"Stay the course. Don't change just to change. Have consistency and routine in the things you do."

—Mark Buderus, Florence (CO) High School

Now that we have figured out why you are coaching, let us talk about your philosophy of building a football program. What is your philosophy? What is your guiding light for building this football program under your management? Your philosophy will be driven by your own mission statement and your reasons for coaching. What is important is that you develop your philosophy and stick with it. That is a common theme that came back from the state champion coaches. It can be summed up by: "Don't change with the wind."

"I would tell another coach to stay the course and stay true to your philosophy and the culture you are trying to create as a coach. Challenge your players on a day-to-day basis, and hold them accountable for their mistakes. Once they buy in to what you are preaching, not only will they be successful football players, but they will be successful people as well."

—Eric Cumba, St. Thomas Aquinas High School (NH)

You need to make a lot of tough decisions about the direction of your program. What kind of offense and defense are you going to run? Are your special teams going to be an important part of your program or just something you do for 30 minutes the day before the game? Are you going to allow kids to miss your off-season program and just come out in August, or are you going to mandate they be there during the tough off-season program?

"The most important aspect of us winning championships is our commitment to consistency. We sell to our kids that winning in football comes from sticking with your system and understanding Chuck Knoll's quote "Champions don't beat themselves; they just do the ordinary things better than their opponent day in and day out."

—Rhett Farmer, Piedmont Academy (GA)

"I would assume every coach wants to win a state championship, but they also need to understand there isn't a perfect system, a definite blueprint, or any other magic pill for a program to achieve success. Coaches should research all aspects of football, decide on their philosophical approach, and then implement a plan. Once the plan is deemed to be fundamentally solid, stick to it. Coaches that waffle will rarely achieve long-term success. In short, do what you believe, and believe what you do. It is fine to tweak systems to fit personnel, but stay within the parameters of your basic philosophy."

—Jeff Gourley, Olathe (KS) South High School

Coaches who have found success in the win-loss column have developed their plan and stuck with it, no matter what anyone else had to say about that plan. The reason that staying the course is so important is because it sets the precedent for the expectations in your program. Everyone knows what to expect from the coach and the football program. There are no surprises. This approach helps your program run like a well-oiled machine. Consistency is key to the success of any type of business; high school football is no different.

> *"Continuity: We run the same offense year after year and all through our 7th through 12th grades. I believe by the time our players become varsity players, they know our system well."*
>
> —Jeff Vanleur, Bridgewater/Emery/Ethan High School (SD)

> *"We do the same thing year after year and don't change much. Our fifth and sixth graders run the same drills and use the same terminology as our kids. Our JV practice with our varsity and learn from our older kids. Our summer program keeps our kids together and is a big part of our team unity."*
>
> —John Schwartz, Mendon (MI) High School

Your Program's Mission Statement

Developing your program's mission statement and/or goals is important because it will serve as a roadmap for your success. It lets everyone in your community know what your program is all about. When I first took over as a head football coach, it was at Linfield Christian in Temecula, California. Our coaching staff was at a clinic in February when our head coach told us he would not be returning. It was a shock to us all. He spoke with me one-on-one and told me that I should apply for the job. I went right to my hotel room and wrote out my mission statement on a napkin. I've used this for eight years as a head coach (Figure 2-1).

Lions Football Will Be Known For:

A—achievement in the classroom by each student-athlete.

C—coaches who teach not only about football but life.

T—their sportsmanship in both victory and defeat.

S—success based not on talent or ability, but a non-negotiable work ethic.

Figure 2-1. Fore's mission statement

As the head coach, these have been the four pillars of my football program for my entire career. I will not hire a coach who doesn't match this short description of what I want my coaches to do. I will not tolerate unsportsmanlike behavior. I will constantly make it a point to let my student-athletes know that their grades are more important than their route running. And, we will always have a very strong work ethic. These guiding principles have served me well over the years. Figure 2-2 is a sample mission statement from Greenville College in Illinois.

If players remain at Greenville College for four years, we will give them:

- A great education
- Great personal attention
- A great family climate

Additionally, if players graduate from Greenville College while participating in our football program, they will have learned how to:

- Be responsible
- Not make excuses
- Not complain

This is who we are and who we want to become.

Figure 2-2. Sample mission statement—Greenville (IL) College

I encourage you to write a mission statement for your program at the end of this chapter. This will help you to stay the course for the long haul. It will serve as the foundation for your success, your blueprint for the future. Without a strong plan in place, you will waver with the wind. Championship coaches have a strong plan, and they don't waver from that plan.

> *"We at St. George's tried to focus on each week. Externally to the team and internally as a staff, we made sure that our week-to-week approach fit our seasonal goal. Our core values for the season were discussed instead of winning. The core values were: truth, respect, loyalty, commitment, and desire. Each day, we talked about our core values, and each Thursday after our walk-through practice, we had a different coach talk about a different topic that was related to our core values. Other than that, we focused on winning daily against ourselves rather than beating our opponent."*
>
> —Brent Hill, St. George's High School (TN)

It Takes Time

> *"It's not that we did something different this year as opposed to other years. It was more about the fact that it takes years to establish a program. We invest more time than other programs in the mental and spiritual components of football."*
>
> —Willie Amendola, Dekaney High School (TX)

"It is a long process that takes a minimum of four years to accomplish."

—Greg Maccarone, Glassboro (NJ) High School

"Success never comes easy. There has to be commitment on your end as a coach to outwork the other coaches in your league, and to constantly improve as a coach through clinics, film study, reading, and visiting with your peers. There also has to be commitment and leadership from your players. They have to want to be successful and be committed to getting up early in the summer to lift, and be willing to sacrifice parts of their personal life for the benefit of the team. I think coaches also must encourage their kids to be athletes and not just football players, and be flexible in that you need to coach to your personnel but keep continuity in your system so that you can adjust on the fly."

—Scott Sparks, Denton (MT) High School

"The year before I took the job, the team was 0-11. We were so bad that our goal was just to improve every day. Over the years, we have never deviated from that, and preach that if every player will get a little better every day—whether it be during practice or off-season—get a little better today and multiply that by 75 players, then we have made progress as a team. Using this approach, we have improved every year, culminating with a 27-2 record the last two years and the state championship this season."

—Chuck Reedy, Goose Creek (SC) High School

"This year in particular, we did not change anything. This year's state title comes from years of commitment in the off-season, focusing on goals set years before. A core of players (along with the staff) buying into a belief system and consistently committing their time to the weight room and each other. This commitment and belief lead to higher performance levels on the field, and more importantly, a confidence and togetherness that were unmatched throughout the season. By the time the state tournament came around, there were no egos on the field. Our sole intention was to work as hard as we could (collectively) on every down (just as we had done for years in the weight room on every rep)."

—Tim McMullen, Letchworth High School (NY)

Believe in Your Schemes

"Stay the course. Believe in what you do and how you do it."

—Hal Lamb, Calhoun (GA) High School

I have spent most of my coaching career in what is called the CIF Southern Section. California is broken down into 10 sections governed by the California Interscholastic Federation. The Southern Section has 13 divisions of 11-man football and two divisions of eight-man football. Because I have been at two small, private Christian schools, I have been in the lowest division, Division 13. These smaller schools are made up of teams with sometimes as few as 15 kids to maybe 30 kids on their varsity teams. Most are in the low 20s. When you have this few kids, it's tough to find that stud quarterback year in and year out. Therefore, I have chosen to run the wing-T offense. I have done pretty well with it.

As an example, in 2005, Capistrano Valley Christian went 0-9. They had a great person playing quarterback, and probably their best option for what they were trying to do—a kid named Nate. Well, for a variety of reasons, Nate threw about 25 interceptions his junior year. I became the head football coach there in 2006. I installed the wing-T. Nate became one of the wings, and we made Andre the quarterback. He had been a running back the year before. The kids all kind of laughed when I told them he was going to be moved to quarterback. They had run a version of the spread offense in their winless 2005 season. He was by no means a spread quarterback. But he was the best wing-T quarterback I have ever had. The kid did a great job for us. Our team went 5-5 that year. From 0-9 (and 2-8 in 2004) to 5-5. That was quite an accomplishment, and I give a lot of credit to the scheme. We just did not have the kids to run a spread offense, but we did have the kids to run the wing-T.

Many coaches in the division tried to run the spread when it was getting very popular. They were throwing their own offense right out the window in order to run something they thought was cool. It is kind of ridiculous to see teams who do not have a quarterback to run the spread offense, or the West Coast offense, trying to do those things. But to many people, the wing-T, the double wing, isn't sexy. Who cares? Find something that will work for your kids, and run it.

"We have done nothing differently. We have been knocking on the door forever, it seems like. We stuck to our beliefs, the biggest one being a platoon system. 45 out of 65 kids played in the state championship game. By doing this, we have developed more kids that are able to contribute. Individual improvement is the name of the game. We get better as the season goes on."

—John Ivlow, Bolingbrook (IL) High School

"I don't think (nor do I want to speak) about what other coaches do or do not do in their programs. At Cedar Grove, we have a philosophy about everything: offense, defense, special teams, practice organization, staff meetings, off-season for players and coaches. These philosophies do not really change over the years. They might be adjusted if we find a better way of doing things, but for the most part they are the foundation of our program. Hopefully, our team gets better each day, and by the time we get to the state playoffs, we are hitting on all cylinders. This season, we started off real strong, winning six straight games and then lost two games in a row before we won our last four. Injuries played a factor in those losses, as did the fact that both teams we lost to were playoff teams in a larger group. I would like to believe, at Cedar Grove, we coach our players up and stay consistent with the philosophy we have developed over the years."

—Ed Sadloch, Cedar Grove (NJ) High School

"Get a system you like, and stick with it. Work hard to improve the details of that system. Do not jump around, adding aspects to a system that may look good to start with. Consistency in a system for grades 9 through 12 is vital."

—Carl Lemke, St. Croix Lutheran High School (MN)

Your Fingerprint

Your program needs to have your fingerprint on it. You need to take ownership of it and make it yours. You can't stay the course with someone else's program. If you have recently taken over a program, or if you do in the future, make sure that you make the program yours. Changing the culture to fit what you are trying to do is critical.

Again, I refer to the 2006 season when I started at Capistrano Valley Christian. Lifting weights was a small part of their fabric before I got there. However, some of the kids did not lift with the team. Some of the stars on the team saw their own personal trainer on their time. This was in South Orange County, where many baseball kids have a pitching coach, a running coach, a fielding coach, a bunting coach, etc. When these two certain kids kept missing practice, I would ask why they were not coming to weights. They said "Coach, we have our own guy we go see. We don't lift with the team because it will hurt us for baseball." I had a choice to make: accept this or mandate they lift with the team. The culture had to be changed; they needed to workout with the team. Sure enough, they were in the weight room with us. It took me sitting them down, and in one case sitting down with one of their parents, to explain my philosophy, and why it was very important that they were lifting weights with us.

> *"This year, in my first year as a head coach, we remade the culture of the program. We implemented a whole new system and created a tempo that the kids have never experienced before. Week after week, we stressed the importance of what we were doing and continued to challenge our young men and raise the level of expectation. As a result, we brought the program to a level that not only our kids but our opponents had never seen, and it was evident on a week-to-week basis."*

> —Eric Cumba, St. Thomas Aquinas High School (NH)

> *"My main piece of advice would be: 'You win with good people.' Surround yourself with players and coaches you can trust and who have the same vision as you do in regard to becoming state champions. Once you have that in place, maintain a consistent level of discipline. Players need to know the level of expectations. In the beginning, you will lose players who you think will help you win because they may be good athletes, but they do not understand what it really takes to be the best. In the long run, you will get the athlete who has a great attitude and understands expectations, and your program will be built to win for the long haul."*

> —Jeff Craddock, Tarboro (NC) High School

Time-Out

1. Are you staying the course with your program? Or are you shifting with the wind and the times? If you are staying with the course, in what ways are you doing it?
2. What is your program's mission statement? I summarized my mission statement with A.C.T.S. How do you summarize your philosophy?
3. Do you feel as though your administration supports your mission statement? If not, what are the roadblocks to making that happen? How can you get them on the same page?
4. What is one example from this past season of how you stuck by your philosophy when push came to shove?
5. What do you think the players in your program would say is your fingerprint on the program? Ask some of them, and write your response here.

3

Coaching the Heart of the Athlete

Courtesy of Coach Cote, Bishop Guertin High School (NH)

"As a coach, I try to make certain that each and every kid knows how much I love and care about him each and every day. The good Lord has blessed us 10,000 times over, and we are extremely fortunate to be in such an awesome profession."

    —Jason Herring, Refugio (TX) High School

"Focus on what is important: the kids. Don't focus on what you don't have, or what your competition does have or the people that say it can't be done. The kids are the reason we are here, and them making plays on game day is what will win a championship."

    —Scott Bailey, Lamar (MO) High School

"The connections are what I feel to be the strongest part of our program. Kids have buy-in, which goes a long way. I develop connections by having team-bonding times besides the weight room or field. … The biggest advice that I could give another coach is: make connections with the kids, and make them understand that you value each and every one of the players."

    —Michael Bates, Little Snake River High School (WY)

My entire mind-set of coaching was changed forever on October 29, 2006. I have always felt like I have done a pretty decent job as a coach in regards to caring about my players and treating them with love and respect. But when my first son was born on that Sunday night in 2006, it really changed my perspective on many things. For those of you with children, you know what I am talking about. It is almost as if you get a new pair of glasses with which to see the world through when you become a parent. That view changed part of my approach as a coach because I suddenly saw all of my players as somebody's baby boy. I sat and held my son at two in the morning, feeding him and thought of him playing football in high school. I wondered who his coach would be and how he would be treated. Would his coaches care about him as a person?

State champion coaches reported to me that one of the most significant aspects of their program was coaching the heart of the athlete. This means seeing your players as more than just pawns on the field on Friday nights. Coaches who see beyond Friday night in their players' lives have a great impact on them for the life of the player. This impact will help to develop character that will last far beyond your four seasons with your players. Giving them tools to succeed not just on the field, but in life as well, will help to develop a championship culture of success.

"The last piece of advice is to build relationships with your student-athletes. Find out what is going on in their lives, what their interests are, and find out what activities outside of football they are doing. And above all, be visible in their other activities. Go to their speech and

debate meets; tell them they ran a good race in track. High-five those when they do well on their math test. When you develop these kinds of relationships, they will play harder for you, they will respect you, and problems outside of football will be minimized."

—Pat Murphy, Capital High School (MT)

"The second thing is to show respect to the players. We at Centralia feel we have a great relationship with the players. Our coaching staff gives respect to the kids, and in return we get it back. I think that is so important in a team. They will run through a brick wall for us; in turn, we will do anything to help our kids."

—Larry Glatczak, Centralia/Wetmore High School (KS)

Putting the Person Before the Player

"As a coach, I believe we must get in the bubble of each player. They must know you care about them as individuals off the field even more than on the field. Once they feel that true caring from you, and that is combined with the passion and commitment in the weight room, they will go to the wall for you and the staff. When your leaders or captains feel this way, it becomes pervasive, and it will lift the whole program."

—Tim McMullen, Letchworth High School (NY)

A few years ago, I had a player come into my office with a few tears after practice one day. He sat down right across my desk from me and looked me right in the eye. He said, "Coach, I just have one question for you. Do you believe in me? Do you believe I can really do this?" Then, a few more tears fell; he got it all out. This kid had never played football before. In fact, he was an international student from Brazil. He is a great athlete and one of the most passionate kids I've ever coached. At the time of this book was written, he was playing junior college football because he loves the game so much.

I looked at this senior in high school sitting across from me in tears and saw a player who desperately needed positive affirmation from his coach, and I had not been doing it. I have never been the type to lie to a kid. I tell them how it is. I do not like blowing smoke up a kid's rear end just to make him feel better, because in the end, that can hurt the kid. I think it is important to be honest, with love and concern. And I was honest with this kid on that day. I said, "I absolutely believe in you. If I didn't believe in you, you wouldn't be in that starting group. We know you can do this. That is why we are constantly on you. We [the coaching staff] believe in you more than you believe in you."

I could tell that my answer was just what he was looking for. We ended up having a great talk and hugged it out as he left my office. It hit me again that day: we as coaches need to continually be reminded that we are coaching people. We are coaching *people* with real emotions. For the most part, these emotions are more than you and I ever dealt with when we played. Kids are different today. We need to focus and refocus on a daily basis in putting the person before the player.

> *"I don't know if we do anything differently than others, but we have assured our players that we truly, genuinely care about all of them. Each of them knows—whether they are a superstar, starter, or practice player—that we are going to treat them equally. What one gets, they all get. My favorite quote, which I tell our coaching staff that we will live by, is: 'They don't care how much you know until they know how much you care.'"*

> —Strait Herron, South Pointe High School (SC)

I love what Coach Herron says about treating his players equally no matter what their status is on the depth chart. This approach is truly putting the person before the player. When you put the person before the player, kids will feel valued. They will feel that you do genuinely care about them. In turn, these kids will buy in to you, the person before they buy in to you the coach. An old adage says, "They don't care how much you know, until they know how much you care." I remind my coaching staff about this a few times a year. Kids are looking for genuine adults who care about them as people. If you are phony and you do not really care about them, they will know, they will see right through you, and they will not care what you know about football. *But*, if your players know that you truly do care about them off the field just as much as you care about them on the field, they will care what you know about football.

That kid in my office, he could have given a rip about my football knowledge. He did not care what I had done in the past as a football coach. He didn't care about my experience as a head coach or my win-loss record. All he cared about that day was that I believed in him. It was all about our relationship. What I realized that day was he needed more of me caring about him as a person, he needed more communication from me off the field, not on the field. He needed that personal connection. So, I worked on that with not only that kid, but others on our team after that meeting.

Coaching Your Kids Beyond Friday Night

Many coaches reported some type of character building program as a part of their football program. They cited this character building as an important aspect of their state championship because it helped to raise the level of commitment to the program. Coaching your kids beyond Friday night means that you are giving them tools to succeed in life, not just on Friday night.

> *"Don't forget to teach beyond the game to your players. You may or may not win championships, but you will at least know you attempted to pour good stuff into your players when you had them. Also,*

remember to build your student leaders and provide them with skills to tackle the upcoming season."

—Frederick Bouchard, Staley High School (MO)

"I believe focusing on character above everything else enabled us to win a state championship. The character of the players outweighs everything else because character enables you to overcome every obstacle, confront every problem, and work together as a team without any personal agenda. In our championship game, we were beaten more than once during the game, but the character of the players would not let them give up or give less than 100 percent of themselves. Character is the ingredient champions are made of, not wins and losses."

—Leroy Willis, Lucas (TX) Christian Academy

Are you coaching your kids beyond Friday night right now? Or is it all about Friday night in your program? What would your kids say if I came to your campus and asked them? Would they tell me that you care about them beyond Friday night? As I mentioned earlier, a few years ago I had a 0-10 season. I am telling you right now that I totally lost focus. All that mattered to me was getting a win, any win, any way possible. I had to get that monkey off my back. It was the worst season of my life, and the kids who played for me will tell you that I was a jerk. I lost the focus that I had for years about putting the kids first. I was on edge the entire season, just grinding and grinding to get a win. I totally forgot about the character-development part of things during that season. If you asked my kids that year, they would have said I did not care about them; I will admit to that right now.

Coaching kids beyond Friday night means that you get to know your kids on an individual basis. It means that you have a personal relationship with your kids. For some of you, that is easy; it comes naturally. For others, it might be a difficult thing. This might be a new concept for some of you. I encourage you to embrace it. Getting to know your players at the person level will be one of the most rewarding things you will ever do. Several years ago, I was asked to officiate the wedding of a former player. Quite honestly, that was one of the highlights of my career, marrying Brad and Christina. That happened because we had a great relationship off the field. When he graduated, we kept in touch. Our relationship started on the football field, but was really developed in my classroom at lunch time. Brad would hang out in my class, and we would talk about life. He knew that I was there for him, and that I cared about him beyond what he could do on Friday nights.

How does getting to know your kids on a personal level lead to winning football games? From my experience, when you invest in your players off the field, they will invest in you on the field. For instance, when you hold them accountable for not being at an off-season weightlifting session, and you have that personal relationship, they will respond in a positive way. If you don't have that relationship, they will usually not respond very positively. If you have deposited into that "emotional bank account" of your players, you can make a withdrawal when you need to. This means you can usually get after your players on the field with whom you are the tightest. I know I'm always the toughest on the kids who I know the best. I know what buttons to push, what buttons not to push. I know what and how to say things to certain players because I've spent the time getting to know them off the field. Coaching the heart of the athlete will help your program on the field.

> *"It goes back to two things for me: relationships with the kids and trust from the kids. I asked my kids to do more things in practice this year, mentally and physically, and because of the relationship I have with them and the trust they have in me, they never hesitated, questioned, or backed down from the challenge."*

> —Terry Ward, Tenaha (TX) High School

In my program one year was a kid named Jordan, who I was getting to know pretty well. I knew he was feeling sorry for himself one day during training camp. If I didn't know him as well as I did, I might have let him off the hook. But I pushed and pushed him that day. He was complaining about leg cramps in his calf. So I got him up on the training table and dug my fist in to his big linemen calves, and I massaged out some of the soreness and stiffness. Then I told him to get back out there and get after it. He was still feeling sorry for himself, so I just kept riding him. I had invested in him outside the field, so I could do that with him. He pushed through practice and thanked me for it years later. As a senior, he talked about that day as a little sophomore when I was hard on him and pushed him to practice when he did not think he could. He pointed to that day as being a game-changer for his football career.

> *"Your players need to know where you stand. What are you willing to do? What would you be willing to sacrifice? Express your true concern for your players. If a young man is willing to go out and lay it on the line for you, you better love them to death. Football is one of the last team sports where players can make ultimate sacrifices. Players need to know that you care. Are you a life-changer as a coach? You can be. Get your players to play to their potential by reaching down into their souls and pull out everything that they have. Leave nothing on the table. Tell them the truth. If they lack effort, tell them. If practice is poor, tell them. Be honest and forthright. Get rid of your personal agenda. Everybody wants to win. All coaches are driven to succeed. It is those coaches who have eliminated their need to win and who focus on the molding of championship people that end up succeeding."*

> —Vincent Lorenzano, Bishop Chatard High School (IN)

Putting a System Into Place

If you haven't figured it out yet, I'm a systems guy. I believe you have to have systems in place to get things done. Systems are just another word for process. What is the process that your program has in place to coach the heart of the athlete. Do you do something on a weekly basis that will help your staff to coach beyond Friday nights? Do you have a process in place to teach character?

I've done this a few different ways over the years. I've spent 10 years at private Christian schools. This meant I had a lot of freedom to share my Christian faith with my players. One way we taught character development was through a weekly Bible study. Some years it would be a part of our film study on Mondays; some years it would happen on Thursday night at our team meal. Some years I have had our kids lead a devotion based on God's word, and some years I have assigned each of our coaches a week to do this. There are a variety of ways to teach faith-based character development if you are at a faith-based institution.

I've seen and heard of coaches putting a system in place to coach the heart of the athlete in a number of ways. A character development program where you focus on one characteristic each week is a great way to go. Focus on characteristics like determination, integrity, trustworthiness, or loyalty. You can have a coach do a 10-minute lesson on what it means to be a determined person. Focus on this theme of determination all week. Try to find some type of drill you can do on the field to teach determination. Have a few kids share during the week about how they've had to have determination some time in their lives. This type of character building program will coach the heart of the athlete. The lessons you impart on your kids will go far beyond Friday night, and just might be some of the most important coaching lessons your kids take away from your program.

One of the greatest ways I've seen our own program coach the heart of the athlete is through our Thursday night team meals. Like many programs do, we go to a family's home after practice on Thursday to have a meal together. At one school where I was, the tradition was for all of the families to come to this meal. So, we would have moms and dads and brothers and sisters, everybody there for the meal. It was a nice tradition. At some point during the night, we would all go in to the garage, or a basement or a side yard, and talk about goals. I stole this idea from one of the greatest high school coaches of all time, Bob Ladoceur of Concord de la Salle. Coach Ladoceur was nice enough to open up his practices to my staff several years ago. I sent my staff up there to watch spring practice for three days. One of the things my guys brought back was their Thursday night goal setting and accountability.

Each kid stands up and shares three goals with his teammates: a practice goal, a game goal, and a weight lifting goal. For instance: a player may say "For my practice goal, I am going to catch 30 balls after practice each day; for my game goal, I am going to catch every ball thrown to me, and for my weight lifting goal, I am going to do two more reps on the clean than I am supposed to." These are all written on an index card. He then picks out a teammate or coach who will hold him accountable to these goals throughout the course of the next week. At the following week's meal, those two kids will stand up, and we will hear a report on those goals the kid made the previous week. Right there before all of his teammates and coaching staff, we will hear if he reached his goals or not. We teach the kids to choose goals that are measurable and attainable and realistic. For a backup receiver to say, "My game goal is to have 100 yards," that is not a realistic goal, so we will challenge him to choose another goal.

What I really love about this process we have put into place is that, most of the time, when a kid fails to meet his goals, it is not a matter of his talent or his ability. It has everything to do with his heart and his attitude. It is interesting to see the correlation between winning and these goal cards. It happens almost all of the time the same way. If we have a week where our kids did not reach their goals, we usually lose. The atmosphere in the room that night, when kid after kid gets up and says, "I failed to reach this goal or that goal," usually matches the atmosphere at practice that week. And that translates to how we play. You see, it all goes back to the heart of the players, and their personal resolve to do their best. If a kid keeps failing to meet his goals, I will pull him aside at a dinner or maybe during the week in my office to ask what is going on. And usually, something is going on in his life that has negatively impacted his resolve on the football field. If you are not doing something like this to get to know your kids, and to hold them accountable to becoming better players and people, I highly suggest you incorporate some type of system in to your program.

> *"I truly believe the one thing that sets our program apart from other programs is our commitment to coaching the heart of the athlete. Most coaches get so caught up in the X's and O's, but they never spend time coaching the heart of their kids. Our program is very involved in the Fellowship of Christian Athletes, and we focus on giving our football team a Christ-centered foundation that will last long after football is over. We pray together, read bible scripture together, and we attend church together once a month as a team. We also spend time together just hanging out as team while having Madden tournaments, playing cards, watching movies, and going bowling as a team. I truly believe the time we as coaches invest in our players off the football field is what drives them to give us so much effort on Friday nights. In today's society, we are seeing more and more kids coming from single-parent homes, where most are single-mother households, so as a coach we have to fill this void as a father figure for our kids. I have players in my home on a consistent basis so they can see what a successful and functional family looks like. Ultimately, what we as coaches should be teaching our kids is so much bigger than just football."*

> —Jeremy Brown, Jefferson County High School (FL)

"While we obviously coach the fundamentals, day in and day out, our staff works diligently on developing the whole person with our players. Our philosophy is Christ-centered and challenges the young men we coach spiritually, socially, academically, and athletically. We teach and model servant-leadership and work hard to foster team chemistry and unity. And just like any great team across America, you've got to have great kids and families and great school support. We've been blessed with both over the years."

—Tommy Lewis, Hilton Head Christian Academy (SC)

Time-Out

1. What is your greatest success in coaching a kid past Friday night? Where is that kid now? How did you have such a great influence on him?
2. "As a coach, I try to make certain that each and every kid knows how much I love and care about them each and every day. The good Lord has blessed us 10,000 times over, and we are extremely fortunate to be in such an awesome profession," said Jason Herring of Refugio (TX) High School. If I came to your campus today, would your players say that you care about them? Why or why not?
3. What programs do you have in place to help you and your staff coach the heart of the athlete?
4. What are three things that you learned from this chapter that you want to implement this coming season?
5. How can *you* do a better job of putting the *person* before the player this next season?

4

The Little Things: Daily Discipline With the Fundamentals

Courtesy of Coach Bouchard, Staley High School (MO)

"'Focus on the little things' is the best piece of advice I ever received as a coach. Take care of the small things that are important (fundamentals, relationships between teammates and coaches), and the big things like winning will come. Be committed to your values and stick with them, even if it costs you games now, because you will win in the future."

—Rick Streiff, Cathedral High School (IN)

Three Little Things, One Big Headache

I will never forget my first away game as a head football coach; it was September 2003. The game was in Hawaii. Not a bad place to travel for a game, is it? We played in the famous War Memorial Stadium on the island of Maui. The NFL's pro bowl was held there for a long time. It was pretty neat, looking at pictures of their locker room and field with all of these NFL players in them when telling our guys where we were going.

I left three very important little things back home in our equipment room in Southern California. It was the absolute last time I forgot any of these three items; I learned a good lesson after that first away game as a head coach. The day before the game, while practicing in helmets, shirts, and shorts, a few kids came asking for the helmet air tool while putting on their helmets before practice. I guess the air pressure in the plane ended up changing the air in their helmets quite a bit. We looked everywhere for it, and we didn't have it. I forgot to pack it. When we got home, I found it right on my workbench in our football office.

We knew that we wouldn't have field goals to practice on for that practice. We used a field right next to the ocean. It was tough to get anyone to focus. So, the first time my kicker practiced kicking field goals was during pre-game. So, he's digging through the ball bag and looks up at me and says, "Coach, where's the tee?" It was in our kicking bag, 2,600 miles away.

I went to one of our equipment trays to get my whiteboard marker out. I always have it with me, in my back left pocket during games. It wasn't there. Sure enough, it was also left in Temecula, on the whiteboard in our office because one of us coaches had used it after our last practice before flying to Hawaii. "What a nightmare," I thought to myself. Every head coach knows the importance of having that marker with you during games to be able to make adjustments with your players right there on the sidelines during the games.

On the flight back to California, I made a list of every single thing that our football program needed for road trips. I put down everything that I could think of that night. Then, with my coaches during the next week, I ran that list by them to see if there was anything I was missing. Sure enough, there were a few things I didn't have on my list. One was the cleats box, a small box we have with a bunch of replacement cleats in case any players break theirs off during games. From that Hawaii game to this day, I've used that same list every Thursday or Friday, the day before our games, to help our staff remember what needs to be brought to the game, and who is responsible for making sure it gets there.

The little things. Little things can make a big, big difference in a football program. And a high school football program has a lot of little moving parts to it. Luckily, we were able to borrow a tee from Baldwin High School that night for my kicker to warm up with. Nevertheless, he was freaking out a little because it was not his normal tee. Can you imagine if it came down to a field goal to win that game? I had a parent run out to buy me a marker for the sideline white board; luckily, I had discovered I was missing it early enough. We also borrowed a helmet pump from our opponent that night. But that meant we had a lot of kids with helmets that did not fit during practice. Some were so bad they had a hard time forgetting about their helmet and focusing for the last practice before the game. Three little things, but each of them added up to get me pretty frustrated. There was no excuse for forgetting this stuff outside of not double-checking, and not having a list as a guide to help me remember everything. My only excuse was that it was my first away game as a head coach.

I have seen little things have much more dramatic effects on a football team: that little D- that turned into an F and kept a kid out of a football game, that little personal foul at the end of a hard-fought game that put a team into field goal range, that starting running back forgetting his cleats in his car back in the parking lot. All of these little things, or even one, can hold a team back from reaching their peak performance.

"We never talk about winning. Winning is a by-product of outexecuting and outworking your opponent. Focus on what you can control, which are the little things: footwork, technique, and off-season training. We are always stressing to our student-athletes to not look at the score board, to trust their teammates, and to trust their opponents. Fans should be able to come to our games at any time and not be able to tell if we are up by 42 or down by 42 points because of our level of play. Our level and intensity of play should be consistent no matter what the score. This attitude takes time to develop. You must constantly coach your athletes on footwork, and doing things perfectly. You must develop an atmosphere in which the athlete is expected to go hard at every snap. Film study is an excellent way to get this done."

—Pat Murphy, Capital High School (MT)

Focusing on Little Things Matters

One of the themes repeated time and again from the coaches I interviewed for this book was focusing on the little things in your program. The little things like fundamentals on a day-to-day basis. You have so many things to focus on as the head coach of your program that sometimes the little things are left undone. Sometimes, we get so consumed with making sure we have every play for every scenario (if you are coaching the offense) that we forget to focus on making sure the quarterback gets the ball right. Or we stop working on the fundamentals like catching and route running as the season goes on. The great programs focus on fundamentals all season long.

I recently read that 50 percent of games in the NFL are decided by eight points or less, basically a touchdown and two-point conversion. That goes to show you how important every inch is in the game of football. We saw Bill Belichick vilified a few years ago in Indianapolis when his team couldn't get a few inches on a fourth-down play. Those inches lead to first downs, which lead to touchdowns, which lead to victories, which lead to championships.

> *"We spent a great deal of time teaching fundamentals early in the season that helped us during our playoff run. We also spend a great deal of time teaching leadership skills that help to build great leaders with great character. Our senior class has great leaders. Work hard on the little things, and be positive throughout the entire season."*
>
> —Seth Stinton, Melissa (TX) High School

> *"Resiliency and attention to detail. We always preach that injuries and depth are critical elements in the game of football, and that it is the most true 'team sport.' Everybody contributes in some way either on offense, defense, special teams, or scout teams, and every player must be ready when his name is called. We got down to our fourth-string tailback in the quarterfinals, and he carried the ball six times for 48 yards and helped us on the game clinching drive. Our quarterback did a hook slide inbounds at the opponent's three-yard line with 1:28 to go that allowed us to score and run the clock out with a five-point lead at the time. We had covered it only during August, and he performed it in late November. We rep anybody that has a chance to play, and we preach readiness in practice. Attention to detail is handled through film study and meetings."*
>
> —Joe Prud'homme, Nolan Catholic High School (TX)

Prud'homme's story is one of my favorites from all of the 2011 season research. The little things matter, don't they? This kid had the presence of mind to practice a very minute detail from something he learned in practice. I've never even thought to practice this during my time as a head coach. But this one little thing helped contribute in a major way to their state championship. The attention to detail, which Coach Prud'homme drills in to his kids, is such a part of his program that it becomes like second nature to the players. They execute the little things on the field because it has been ingrained in them that the little things matter.

"I feel we did the little things right. You can't just coach the big picture, because the big picture is made from several little pictures."

—Jon Ellinghouse, Sierra Canyon High School (CA)

"I think something we did very well this year was to get our kids to buy into concentrating on the details and little things. Little things make big differences. Focusing on the little things helps with execution, penalties, and preparing kids in making plays. Hopefully, these all lead to real life. Selling the kids on hard work, commitment, and selflessness builds teams and young men. Relating character to life as a husband, father, employee, and person of faith helps young people understand the commitments they are making in sports is helping them grow as a person. If the kids can concentrate on little things, they have the ability to focus on the details of every play and every assignment. This started from day 1 during stretches, warm-ups, and everyday drills."

—Andy Lowry, Columbine High School (CO)

"I would advise any coach to fix your team's performance one play at a time. Block and tackle your opponents, yes, but typically poor performances are a result of individuals not fixing the details of their position. If you can fix your own technique weakness, you will expose the weakness of your opponents."

—Bruce Kozerski, Holy Cross High School (KY)

Five Little Things to Focus on in Your Program

Knowledge of Rules

When was the last time you had an official come in to talk with your players about the new rules for the upcoming season? Or just to go over some of the big things that get called a lot. I learned this from a college coach at a clinic. He talked about how they brought in a few officials every year to talk with his team and staff about the new rules, and the points of emphasis. That was in 2005. Ever since then, I have brought in one of the top officials in our area to talk with my team for 30 minutes during our training camp. Then, they stay afterward with a few other officials and come work our scrimmage.

I love being able to hear firsthand from these guys exactly what the new rules are, and exactly what they are (and are not) looking for on certain calls like clipping, blocking in the back, and holding. It is great for our offensive line to hear from an experienced official where they are going to get in trouble and where they will be okay. This is one of those little things that you can do to help your players succeed. Plus, it will give them an appreciation for the officials, which I think is important. Contact your local officials association; I am sure they will be happy to help. I have never had a hard time getting them out to our training camp before the season.

Accountability for Little Things

I was at a St. Margaret's High School practice a few years ago. It was in December, and my team was done for the year. Their coach, Harry Welch, invited any coaches from our league who were done playing to come out to practice. At the time, they were on their way to an amazing 42-game winning streak, and a first state championship for the school. Coach Welch has now won three state championships with three different schools in California.

One thing I learned that day watching his team practice was about accountability for the little things. They must have kicked about 20 point-after-touchdown kicks. I mean, we are very late in the season, in December, and he is yelling about a wing in the protection scheme who had his feet about three inches from where they should have been. He made them kick over and over and over until this one kid got his positioning right. It's one of the reasons he has had so much success, paying attention to a kid's feet, he demanded perfection with the placement of these feet.

One tool that Coach Welch uses to ensure his team is being held accountable for the little things is that he makes them run. If a play does not go right, they stop what they are doing right then and there, and all of the kids run to a sideline. Then, they sprint to the other sideline and back. The result is instant accountability for the little things.

> "Accountability is the most important aspect of our championship season. Work on it with players, coaches, and yourself every day."
>
> —Harry Welch, Santa Margarita Catholic High School (CA)

> "We focus on the little things in football. We run the single-wing offense and really pay attention to detail and executing the plays to perfection."
>
> —Larry Glatczak, Centralia/Wetmore High School (KS)

> "Athletes carried out each assignment to a high degree of excellence. It is developed through consistency and repetition."
>
> —Carl Lemke, St. Croix Lutheran High School (MN)

> "'Greatness is uncommon; therefore, it will not be achieved by the common man.'" is the motto we lived by in 2011. We had to get everyone in the program to strive for greatness in what they do every day. As coaches, we refused to let them settle for just getting by. We didn't let them just blend in. Every player was held accountable to stand out and make a difference. They were not allowed to be common. Day by day, we got better and better—until we got to a point where we couldn't be beaten."
>
> —Richard Morgan, Oscar Smith High School (VA)

"Our goal from the beginning was to improve every day. Working on something to be better than the day before, our goal was to defend the state title and to play December 3 in the championship game—a goal we reached together."

—Mike Young, Central Catholic High School (WV)

Daily Practice Preparation

"I'm not sure we do anything completely unique. We try to do what we do. We believe in being fundamentally sound in all three phases of the game. I think we do an outstanding job in preparation week-to-week as well as year-round. Then, taking it from the whiteboards and film room onto the field. I think we run an extremely efficient practice; it is very uptempo with a tremendous number of reps. We believe that our attention to detail during the week and our number of reps allow our players to understand the game plan and play fast."

—Pat Rice, Waunakee (WI) High School

How often do you sit down with your staff to prepare for practice? Do you just run the same practice plan throughout most of the year? I think one of the keys is making sure to prepare for practice. No coach I have worked with has done a better job of this than one of my defensive coordinators named C.J. Del Balso. I know many programs out there do this, but I never had before. He would sit down and prepare the scout offense plays, put them in the exact order that I would need to run them. I ran the scout offense, so he would send me a document with the plays in an order he wanted to see them. This made sure that we were hitting the stuff in practice that we would see Friday night. He would have the cards in order of the percentages that the team would call the plays. It was all broken down very well to prepare our kids. It is one of those little steps that you can take that will lead to better defensive play.

Like all good coaches, he and his defensive staff would break down the plays from about three games of our upcoming opponent, and then put that breakdown in to stats. What is the percentage of times we will see this play from this formation type of thing. Our teams were prepared so well defensively because of this. He would have me run plays on the scout team during the week in the same proportion that the kids might see them on Friday night. Do you spend this kind of time preparing for practice, or do you just go out and practice? Our staff would usually sit down in February to schedule our offensive installation calendar for August. It takes time to practice right. But from reading the feedback from coaches, you can't overlook the little things like practice preparation and expect to have success on Friday night.

"I think we spend more time on ourselves. We are not a big, athletic, or imposing team. Our edge has to be execution. We must outexecute our opponent. Our kids really bought into that this year in all phases of the game. When we needed it most, we seemed to execute at our very best."

—Bob Godsey, Hartselle (AL) High School

Your Equipment

Equipment was an area I was not prepared for my first year as a head coach. During one of our first games that year, we had a chinstrap break on one of our starting backs. We ran the wing-T, so each back is so important. We were scrambling for a chinstrap that would fit in the middle of the chaos of a game. I did not have an extra chinstrap anywhere, so we just took one off of a kid's helmet who was not playing and gave it to the starter. This was not the best solution, was it? What if that backup had to go in the game?

I learned two very valuable lessons that night, two of those little things that can save big headaches down the line. Number one, have a dad volunteer as your equipment manager for games. Maybe it is not a dad, but get somebody on the sidelines who will serve your team in this capacity. They need to know their way around a screwdriver, and not be afraid to be in the chaos of the game, and the pressure that can come with that. The best equipment manager I ever had was a dad named Dale Hector. Dale thought of things that I never did. He was great at being one step ahead of our staff on the sidelines during games. He would be running out to get a kids helmet if it flew off before I could even turn around and find him to go fix the helmet.

The second thing, pack an extra equipment bag for your games. In this bag, make sure to have at least two backups of everything, if not more. Two extra sets of shoulder pads, two extra game pants, two extra game jerseys, four extra thigh pads, four extra knee pads, etc. Kids will surely forget something, and if you are traveling, this bag is a lifesaver. During a game, if something is broken or missing, this bag will be indispensible.

Special Teams Personnel Chart

Some things you learn just by doing. In my second year of coaching this great sport, I learned about creating a special teams personnel chart. I was coaching the junior varsity team at Fallbrook High School and was put in charge of a few of the special teams.

In one of the very first games that season, I lost a linebacker named Craig to an injury, and never even realized it. I was with the offensive linemen on the whiteboard at the bench. I was not watching the defense. Next thing I know, we are on kickoff return. I am counting the kids in the huddle, and Craig is not there. I am yelling for Craig, and one of our coaches tells me he is hurt, points toward the trainer's table. Sure enough, shoulder pads and helmets are off. What do I do? Grab the first kid I see and tell him to get on the field. He is strapping on his helmet asking "What do I do, Coach?" as he is running out on to the field. "Just block somebody," I yell out at him. How well prepared was this kid? How prepared was I? Was I cultivating a championship program with being unprepared like this?

"I would prepare the same whether your goal is a state championship or to finish with a .500 record. It is the preparation and consistency within your program that will cultivate the championship success."

—Keith Croft, Bishop Hendricken High School (RI)

A little thing—a special teams personnel chart would have helped me in this situation. My special teams personnel chart has the list of all five special teams rosters, and their backups. We go over this every Monday during walk-through. I stand at the five-yard line, while the team is on the end line in the end zone. I yell out, "Kickoff team." My whole team yells out, "Kickoff team." I have them do that so they are active listeners. If they are not on it, I will hold them accountable. The 11 kids on the kickoff team come out to the goal line. I count them by calling out their names and having them respond with a "Here." This gets everyone on the same page as far as who is on what team.

If a player gets injured during the week, we can cross him off the chart and put in his backup. Maybe we want a different returner for one certain game; we just slide him in and remove the other kid. I keep this on the computer and literally print a new one out with my practice plan every practice.

I have it with me on Friday nights. It's laminated back-to-back with my play call sheet. If the team doctor tells me a kid is done for the night, it's very easy to go down the alphabetized lists of special teams and find every special team that "Wilson" is on; I then write a line through his name, and find his replacement. I write the position of Wilson next to that name to remind me who has taken his place.

Figure 4-1 is a sample of one of my special teams personnel charts. It is just three columns of five total columns.

Kick Return	All-State	Return Punt
Burgin: 1	Bautista: 2	Bautista: R2
Caines: D	Burgin: 1	Burgin: R3
Clark: 1	Caines: D	Caines: L2
Mills: 2	Clark: 1	Clark: L3
Hahs: 1	Fages: 1	Hansen: R1
Raftery: 2	Hubby: 2	Hubby: C
Backups listed below the starters.		

Figure 4-1. Sample special teams personnel chart

Time-Out

1. What did you learn from this chapter that you can immediately apply to your football program?
2. What is one thing that your program does very well in regards to the little things?
3. What is something that your program can do better in regards to the little things?
4. I spoke about several game day little things in this chapter. What is a game day little thing that you want to focus on this coming season?
5. California Sierra Canyon's head coach Jon Ellinghouse said, "I feel we did the little things right. You can't just coach the big picture, because the big picture is made from several little pictures." What do you need to do better to do the little things right? Do you need to strengthen your view of the little pictures, or do you do a good job of seeing those?

5

Developing a Work Ethic: Teaching Your Team to Put in the Time

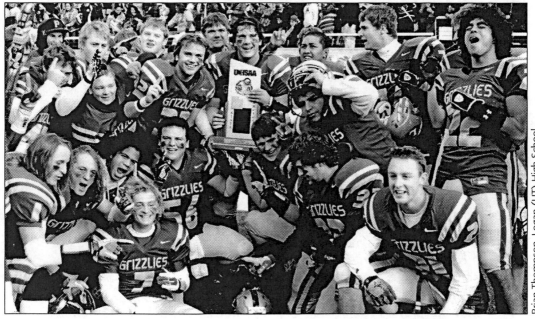

Brian Thompson, Logan (UT) High School

"Keep the vision alive with a great work ethic, and have the ability to persevere."

—Hal Wasson, Southlake Carroll Senior High School (TX)

"We believe a program needs an identity to be successful. We build ours in the weight room the entire year."

—Randy Dreiling, Hutchinson (KS) High School

"The most important part of our team this year was their work ethic, specifically with the strength and conditioning. It was developed as a program from the winter, into the summer and through the season. It helped to keep us healthy and focused."

—Keith Croft, Bishop Hendricken High School (RI)

"I believe we get a competitive edge during our off-season training program. We work extremely hard in our off-season, and our weight lifting/speed development program is run just like a practice. The players are pushed to extreme levels, and a total commitment to our program is required. Every class at Tarboro High wants the chance to become state champions, and they are reminded on a daily basis that only one team in the state will be the best. Never let your opponent outwork you on any given day. Our phrase is: "Somebody is going to get better today; it might as well be Tarboro.""

—Jeff Craddock, Tarboro (NC) High School

"The biggest thing we do differently is that, every day throughout the year, it is important to us to develop as football players and as men. We try harder on a year-round basis because it means a lot to us. … We are 73-2 and have won the state championship the last five years, not because we know something that others don't or have some unique scheme. We do believe in our schemes. We are a high-speed offence that snaps the ball as soon as the official sets the ball. We are a complete two-platoon team, although we are a public school with only 400 boys in the school. We will have 160 of them out for football. All the coaches are speed and strength coaches, and they all work with our players year-round. Our players try harder on a year-round basis than players at other schools. If anything but that last sentence is emphasized, then my message on how to be a consistent state champion is missed."

—Dale Mueller, Highlands High School (KY)

"The most important aspect to this year's team was phenomenal work ethic, character, and athleticism. We had a group of seniors who refused to be outworked or outplayed each and every week. You cannot win unless your kids are 100 percent committed year-round. For instance, our kids don't drink pop. Speed, strength, and proper rest and nutrition are the three pieces of the triangle we focus on most. Have your kids play as much football as they can in the summer, 7-on-7s, attend one to two team camps, and have the seniors set up some captain's practices. Don't make your kids feel like they're locked in a position like a robot. Teach them to think for themselves so that they do not have to think at all on the field. Offensively, you have to save things for the tournament. Defensively you have to be willing to adjust, and always be flexible. They work our speed training regularly and lift with excitement."

—Tim Brabant, Carsonville-Port Sanilac High School (MI)

Without a doubt, the number-one answer from the 2011 state championship head football coaches when asked what they did differently than the other schools in their league, section and state was their work ethic, and specifically their off-season program. These coaches were *convinced* that nobody worked harder than their program did. Championship programs develop their football players on a year-round basis. Those who fail to do so will fall behind the teams who are preparing themselves 12 months a year.

Develop Your Year-Round Philosophy

"We provided the structure and program for our players to work their tails off. Hard work equals success."

—Mark Del Percio, Middletown (DE) High School

What is your off-season philosophy? What do you do with your kids when football is over? Have you been able to sit down with your staff and develop your philosophy? It is critical that you have a philosophy for the off-season. Your philosophy will need to be supported by your athletic director and principal.

Some things to consider when developing your philosophy for the off-season include:
- Do you support student-athletes playing multiple sports?
- If you do, will those kids lift during their basketball or baseball season?
- Have you spoken with the other head coaches at your school about your off-season program?
- Do the athletic director and principal support a year-round off-season program?

- What if a kid wants to join the school play, which consists of three to four hours of after-school preparation? Will you allow your football players to participate in that?
- How do you continue to monitor their grades in the off-season, and what effect does that have on their participation in your off-season program?
- Will you give the kids some time off right after your season? Or do you get right back at it?
- What kind of program are you going to use for developing strength and conditioning?
- What about family vacations, church mission trips, etc. during the summer? What is your policy regarding students who miss three weeks for a once-in-a-lifetime trip on an African safari with their grandparents?
- What about during finals week? Are you going to have the kids in the weight room and on the field during this week?
- Are you going to pay your coaches extra money to help you with the off-season program?

As you can see, many, many items need to be tackled and wrestled with to help shape and determine your philosophy of your off-season program. My policy as a head football coach has always been that if you are not playing another sport in the off-season, your tail needs to be in the weight room, preparing your body for the next season. When many of you reading this book played football, in the 1970s, '80s, and '90s, most kids played many different sports. Over the years, this has changed. I still think it is best for the student-athletes to play as many sports as they can. Will this slow their preparation for your sport, for football? Perhaps it will. Perhaps it will not. That is a philosophy that you will have to determine for your program. How will you handle multi-sport athletes? It can be a sticky issue with the other head coaches on campus. No matter the case, you need to make sure that everyone is on the same page: from other coaches, to the players, to the administration, to the parents of your football players.

> *"The advice I would give to other coaches is that the season does not begin in August; it really begins after the last season ends. Now, some kids do other sports, and that is okay; as a matter of fact, I push for that. However, if they are not in a sport, I try to get them in a weight room and/or to study film. I get them to understand that the season is won out of season, not during. If you want to win a state championship, this is what it takes."*
>
> —Michael Bates, Little Snake River Valley High School (WY)

> *"Strength: weight training for physical strength is a must, but so is competing—for overall strength. Our most valuable players were all multiple sport athletes. The one or two kids that did not really start for other teams (in all cases, they were kids that had injuries and were thus not able to play a winter or spring sport last year) were valuable*

cogs in the wheel, but the true strength (spiritual, physical, mental) came from the kids that had competed in varsity sports for three (or four) years in more than one sport. As I mentioned earlier, patience was the key for us."

—Ed Homer, Christchurch (VA) High School

Raising the Bar

"The most important factor in our championship season is the fact that our kids bought into what we were trying to do. When you are in a new situation, change isn't always welcomed, but we were fortunate enough to be in a great situation. On a day-to-day basis, our football players were challenged to make them themselves better, and we never took a day off from stressing that philosophy. Whether it was finishing a run or a block in a team period, being a good teammate and giving a quality look during an individual rep or knowing all the answers to the questions during a film session, we raised the level of expectation, and the kids met us head on."

—Eric Cumba, St. Thomas Aquinas High School (NH)

"I think our off-season program really got us over the top mentally and physically. Mentally, I think our kids believed they could beat anybody because of the work they put in during the off-season."

—Hal Lamb, Calhoun (GA) High School

In 2006, I took over as the head football coach at Capistrano Valley Christian School in San Juan Capistrano. They were 0-9 in 2005 and 2-8 in 2004. My first year there, we went 5-5; we lost two games on the very last play of the game. We were that close to going 7-3 after a winless season. The number-one obstacle I faced was the lazy work ethic. The kids just were not used to working hard. They were not used to lifting weights during the season, they were not used to watching film, and they were not used to practicing hard. But as we started to win, they started buying in. They started to see the fruit of their labor.

The kids were used to losing over the last couple of years. I don't think they had a winning season in the four years prior to me taking over. I told them at the first meeting that I have gone to the playoffs every year as a head coach and that it would not change this year. Many kids came up to me afterward, asking if I *really* thought that we could go to the playoffs. We started talking about going to the playoffs and winning right away. Do not shy away from that. My kids bought into that right away. When they knew that I believed we could win, they believed we could win. You have to set the bar high, the kids will jump over it. By the way, we did go to the playoffs.

Work Smarter, Not Harder—Have a Plan

"I am not sure exactly what we do differently than other teams in our state, but I do know that we have a 12-month calendar that we use to ensure we are doing something every day as coaches and players to improve. We break those 12 months up into pre-season, season, and post-season, and we have specific goals that we want to accomplish during each of those periods. We use the old philosophy regarding "Plan your work, then work your plan," and everybody in our program has bought into this approach."

—Kevin Wright, Carmel (IN) High School

"The chemistry of a team is developed in the months of training that lead to a season. The leadership of our coaches and seniors established a great foundation for our team as we worked in the winter months. The work ethic that results from our training in the off-season has been a core of our success for many years. It allows our players to push each other to new competitive standards and develop a toughness level that will allow them to conquer the adversities that a season brings."

—Kevin Wallace, Bowling Green (KY) High School

"Revised strength and conditioning program was the most important aspect of our Championship team this year."

—Joe Kinnan, Manatee High School (FL)

"Weight lifting is the major component to our success. In our conference, if you are not strong enough, you will get pounded. We play in the toughest nine-man conference in the state of South Dakota. We developed the importance of lifting by making it the sole criteria for if a player letters or not. Quarters of play have nothing to do if a player letters or not. Who is to say that a freshman hasn't worked as hard as a senior, just because the senior plays more? Our players have to lift 90 percent of the scheduled lifting days during the season. We lift two days a week during the season. Once they are hooked, getting them into the weight room during the summer is easy."

—Lenny Schroeder, Canistota (SD) High School

You can find probably a hundred different philosophies on how to develop strength and conditioning in your football program. Are you going to use a system like Bigger Faster Stronger? Are you going to use kettlebells? Are you going to use Olympic lifts only? No Olympic lifts? Do you want to add bulk? Or speed? Or both? Are you going to lift and run three, four, or five days a week? Before or after school? Are you going to hire a strength and conditioning coach, or do it yourself?

"The most important aspect of our program is our strength program. We lift weights throughout the off-season, summer, and in season. We probably lift as much as we practice. We had two injures out of 65 guys over a 14-game season. Those two guys only missed a combined four games."

—John Ivlow, Bolingbrook (IL) High School

"Incorporated sequencing as our strength training program. Sequencing is an innovative strength training program developed by Dr. Matt Rhea, the main focus of which is training the central nervous system. We also trained metabolically by using football modeling."

—Mike Favero, Logan (UT) High School

"First off, we had an exceptional group of kids with a senior class of strong leaders who have been talking about, believing in, and building toward the goal of a state championship since they were seventh graders. This past off-season, we challenged them to make that dream a reality by dedicating, working, and pushing themselves at a level they never have before with the help of an outside trainer and "agent of change," Rick Cugini. This intense off-season not only prepared us physically for the 15-week run it takes to win a state title in Ohio, but more importantly it built us up mentally and developed our character (or, as we called it, 'heart power') to a point that no opponent, circumstance, or challenge ever seemed too hard or caused us to doubt ourselves."

—Joe Harbour, Norwayne High School (OH)

As you can see, again, a lot of different things need to be thought through regarding your strength and conditioning program. What is important, and what my research shows, is that you find something for *you* that works, and stick with it. Sit down and develop your plan for the weight room. More research is out there than you will ever be able to read regarding how to make kids bigger, faster, and stronger. You can talk with 10 different head coaches in the same part of the state, and they might all do things differently. The absolute key is to have your staff and kids work smarter in the off-season program, not necessarily harder.

Develop your plan, track the progress of your kids, and evaluate what you are doing every year. How will you know that your program is working if you aren't tracking the progress of the kids? If you don't see vast improvements in their 40-yard dash times from January to June, you probably aren't working smarter. Your kids might be working hard, but are they getting better? I'm a big believer in stats. Numbers never lie. I've been surprised to talk with coaches that don't really track their kids' progress at all. I think tracking is very important to do so that you can continually improve your program. This approach is part of working smarter, not harder.

"One of the unique things that we do at Bishop Hendricken is an off-season point program where athletes earn points not only for weight lifting, but also for good grades, community service, and playing other sports. This allows us to not only monitor our students during the off-season, but also encourages them to actively engage in the school community."

—Keith Croft, Bishop Hendricken High School (RI)

Hold Kids Accountable

"Acceleration program: We run an acceleration program during the summer months, in which we have a high percentage of our players participate. Last year, we had 97 percent of our players attend."

—Jeff Vanleur, Bridgewater/Emery/Ethan High School (SD)

"What separated us from the rest of the teams was our commitment to our off-season strength and conditioning program. We had 100 percent commitment two hours per day, five days a week for the entire summer. Our players were much stronger, faster, and polished than the players on the other teams we played. Our ability to maintain our focus and efforts on our team philosophy of 'One rep, one day, one team, and one week at a time' really gave us the psychological edge on our opponents throughout the season."

—Tim Brabant, Carsonville-Port Sanilac High School (MI)

One of the absolute musts in your off-season program is holding the kids accountable to being there and working. You need to have an attendance chart and use it on a daily basis. This tool will help you to stay on top of your kids, and know where they are, who *is* and *is not* working. Depending on the size of your program, keeping an eye on your team in the off-season may be a challenge. That is why keeping accurate records is important. What happens if a kid bails out on lifting a few days a week? What does your philosophy say? What if mom and dad call and excuse him because of out-of-town relatives visiting?

Accountability by *you*, the head coach, in the off-season will build a work ethic in your team. If kids know that they can miss the workouts, and nothing will happen, they will miss the workouts. If they know that you are serious about your policies regarding the off-season program, that you really are going to hold them accountable, they will take it as serious as you do. What are you going to do when one of your star players tries to buck the system?

I had an NCAA Division 1 kicker in my program in my first few years as a head coach. He also played some at receiver. He had a tremendous sophomore year, his first year ever playing football. Our head coach moved, and I took over the program. So, he tested my policy, a few kids did. He failed to come to anything during the summer, but still wanted to play. Our policy was that if you were in town, you work out. If you are on a vacation with your parents or a mission trip with your church, all you had to do was notify me in writing ahead of time. It was a simple policy. I've always supported kids spending time with their families and churches during the summer. But the kids and families must communicate with me so I know what is going on. Well, this kid wasn't around all summer. He missed the first day of training camp, two practices. He showed up the next morning, and wanted to practice. Our team was stretching, he was late. Everyone knew what our policy was, and it was going to be tested for the first time under my watch as a head coach. Would I succumb to a star athlete, or hold to our policies?

We didn't let him play. He said, "Hey, Coach, I heard you need a kicker." The whole team was watching now. "Nope, we have a kicker," I responded. He left. At the next water break, I had five or six of my leaders come up to say things like "Thank you" and "I am glad you did that because he does not care about the program." Our special teams suffered that year; I am not going to lie. Our kicking game was not as good as it was the year before. However, the expectations were now set, and every kid knew that our coaching staff meant business in regards to our off-season program. If you are not committed, you do not play, period. That kid came back very strong the next season. He hardly missed a day all off-season. He had a fantastic senior year, was recruited by several schools, and went on to kick in the Sugar Bowl a few years later. The ending to that story was a great one.

More Thoughts on Work Ethic

"Others do it, but we feel like we have one of the best off-season and boot camps around. We teach our kids to push past their comfort zone and think about their teammates more than they do themselves.

"You have to convince your kids that the only way to be successful in life and in football is hard work. You have to convince them that we are going to be the hardest working team in the state. You have to convince them that, on Friday nights, they have to be willing to play harder, faster, and more physical than the opposing team."

—Thomas Sitton, Chapel Hill High School (TX)

"Kids made a year-round commitment to football."

—Billy Kirch, Waverly/South Shore High School (SD)

"Teach players how to work. I think kids today need to be taught how to work hard. It seems to be a lost characteristic that kids do not learn. Also gaining trust for your program. Getting players to trust in the coaching staff, their teammates, and themselves."

—Jeff Vanleur, Bridgewater/Emery/Ethan High Schools (SD)

"Most of the teams now are doing what we do, which is putting time into the weight room and attending summer team camps. A few years ago, we were one of the only teams that did this, but now everyone has tried to copy what we do in the off-season."

—Mark Gibson, Bismarck (ND) High School

"Time. You have to go the extra mile at all times: winter, spring and especially summer. I don't have much of life during the summer. I am either running young-aged camps in town, taking our team to different team camps, and spending six hours a day in the weight room. You must make the commitment if you expect your kids to."

—Mark Gibson, Bismarck (ND) High School

Time-Out

1. I interviewed more than 100 state champion head football coaches for this project. Their number-one answer to the question "What did your program do differently than others in your league, section, and state that led to a state championship?" was: work ethic. These coaches were *convinced* that nobody worked harder than their program did. Championship programs develop their football players on a year-round basis. Are you *convinced* that nobody works harder than your program in your league, section/division, and state? Why or why not?
2. What two aspects of your program need a better work ethic?
3. From what you have read and learned during this chapter, what are three things you are going to commit to do in order to improve the work ethic in your program?
4. Is your staff committed to increasing the work ethic in your program? Which coach is the weakest link in this area? Will you be able to get him on board with a renewed vision to increase the work ethic? Or do you need to get rid of him?
5. How about your players? Are there any players in your program that are roadblocks to increasing the work ethic? If you raise the bar, do you think they will jump over it? Are you prepared to lose them?

6

Leadership: Creating Influence and Direction

Courtesy of Coach Kinnan, Manatee High School (FL)

"We have a very unique training camp right before the season that develops team unity, leadership, and mental toughness, along with focusing on our core values of faith, family, character, and attitude. We train on sand dunes, ski slopes, and trails, and we have team-building exercises. Our seniors took charge from the beginning and made it our most successful camp to date. Their leadership and attention to detail was tremendous, and it carried us throughout the season."

—Mike Boyd, Nouvel Catholic Central High School (MI)

"We had an incredible sense of unity, leadership, and confidence within our program this year. It can be attributed to the group of seniors we had leading and their willingness to listen to their coaches, and the group of underclassmen who were willing to follow."

—Don Julian, Sheridan (WY) High School

"The key for us was a great attitude and leadership from our seniors. They led us in the off-season and made our weight program a significant role in our success."

—Neil Minton, Colleton Prep Academy (SC)

"Each year, you hope to get the most from each player, and in turn give them the best possible experience. Requiring selflessness in practice is difficult given the volume of expectations on their time. Football must be important to all the players all the time, but they are still kids. It comes down to a critical mass of leaders, and those leaders usually have to be seniors. If your senior class is not focused on success (demanding full effort and attention from the team as much as possible all season long), you will have difficulty with team climate. This year, we had a significant number of leaders in the senior class, so that when one or two players had bad days, they did not take the whole team with them. The general climate of all practices was both positive and productive. The juniors did not challenge the leadership of seniors. If they tried, they stuck out as outliers. The seniors on my team were in control; we had three captains and tried to focus on them being punctual and focused, and then demanding the same from their teammates."

—Ed Homer, Christchurch (VA) High School

"The most important aspect would have to be the leadership from our seniors. Everyone bought into the conditioning and team concept because everyone saw our seniors working as hard as they could to just win. No one came into the season with a preset agenda. Just to win and have fun playing."

—Ray Steele, Indian River High School (DE)

Without a doubt, one of the absolute most popular responses I received from coaches had to do with leadership. It was the third-most popular answer behind work ethic and developing your program. We have all had teams with great leadership, and we have all had teams with poor leadership. Fortunately for today's coach, leadership development is commonplace. Countless "leadership gurus" offer a hundred different philosophies. Yet, you can still have a vacuum of leadership on your football team. The question for you to think about is: "What am I doing to develop leadership on my football team?"

Do you have a plan in place to create leaders? I am very convinced that leaders are not born; they are made. If your program has a lot of history and tradition, if you have been there for 10 years, you are more apt to have a great system of leadership in place. The older kids teach the younger kids how to do things, and so on. You have spent a considerable amount of time over the last decade in developing a program where kids probably step up when the seniors graduate. If you are in a larger program with 30 kids per grade level, you probably have an easier time finding leaders. However, if you are in a smaller program, you have to work harder to find and develop leadership.

I think the hardest thing in developing leadership at the high school level is that it seems like the cyclical nature of high school football can end up hurting you if you do not have an intentional plan in place. What usually happens is a strong class of leaders comes through. The kind of class that, as freshmen, you know they were special. They probably outperformed your sophomores on different levels. When they are together as a group on the junior varsity team, they lead the freshmen, so that specific freshmen class does not develop their own leaders. They become followers. By the time they are juniors, they have fallen right in line with following those boys right above them. Once those seniors graduate, and the juniors take over, a leadership vacuum results. They have not been depended on as leaders. They have not been developed as leaders. So, they look around and do not take initiative. However, if you have a system in place to develop leaders all the way through, then hopefully you will have a seamless transition of leadership from one class to the next.

The plan that I have used for eight years as a head football coach is a player committee. This player committee has usually consisted of four seniors, three juniors, two sophomores, and two freshmen. We vote each January for the player committee. You only vote for the players in your class. (Freshmen are voted in after training camp in August.) Coaches must verify the voting of the team. There have been some years where our coaching staff did not agree on the votes of the players, and some years where we could have told you how the exact votes will go.

The purpose of the player committee is to be a voice. They are a voice from the coaching staff to the players and the players to the coaching staff. They help to develop our policies and procedures, set the off-season calendar, help with discipline decisions that are not spelled out in our playbook expectations, help design our spirit wear, etc. I meet with this group of kids on a weekly basis, usually either at lunch or before school. I have spent most of my career at a private Christian school, and so I have used different books from Christian authors regarding developing leaders. We have examined the leadership lessons of Jesus; we have studied the leadership lessons of great men and women in the Old Testament. I have also used secular books during this leadership development time.

The point is this: I have been pouring into these kids for eight months by the time training camp comes. They have gotten to know me on a personal level, and vice versa. I can tell when one of them shows up a little down for practice. I will usually go to one of the other kids and tell them, "Hey man, Jordan is in a bad mood right now. You better chat with him about making it through this practice with a positive attitude." My player committee has been the central place where I have spent time developing leadership. It has been my format, my plan.

I hold these kids to a very high standard. They set the pace. A few years ago, I had a kid voted onto the committee that I really questioned. One of my coaches was really fired up that I allowed him on the committee because he did not exhibit many qualities of leadership that we wanted in our kids. But we had just lost a bunch of key leaders, and now this specific group saw him as one. I had a long talk with this coach and explained part of my philosophy: if the kids think another kid is a leader, but we do not, we have to understand he is a leader, period. He might not be a good leader, but he is a leader because others are following him. That took me a few years to figure out, but once I understood it, it really helped me. I did not get frustrated anymore when kids followed someone I thought they should not. I worked harder to get that kid in line with our program.

This certain kid ended up getting kicked off the player committee just three meetings in. Can you believe that? He did not even make it out of February. Why? Because he was late to our second meeting. We warned him not to be late again. It is part of holding our leaders to a higher standard. I told him, "If you cannot get here at 6:30 a.m. on time, aim to get here at 6:15." He blew us off. When I say "us," I mean the other players on the committee. The very next meeting, he missed entirely, without letting any of us know. Simply put, he was testing us. He was the most talented player on the team, hands down. He did not think we would remove him from the player committee. But we did. It sent a message to the whole team that leadership was important.

That kid ended up quitting football altogether that year. He bent under the pressure of our off-season expectations. The other kids around him, his peers were buying more and more into our program, and becoming great leaders. They were constantly calling him out regarding his participation and his effort. He could not handle it, so he quit. Imagine the best kid in your school not playing. It was hard for me to take. But I noticed something very quickly: the kid was a cancer. It was good to have him gone. Everyone kind of breathed a sigh of relief. And how did we do that season? We won the school's first league championship in eight years.

Five Tools to Develop Leadership in Your Program

Ongoing Leadership Training

"We had great leadership from our student-athletes. Whenever I've had great leadership on our team, our success followed. We do leadership training with our upcoming seniors, and we talk about using those skills regularly. Our senior group was on point, and they bought into that concept. We will continue to work on building our student leaders on a regular basis."

—Frederick Bouchard, Staley High School (MO)

"This is the first year that I can remember when we had good strong leadership in every position group. That is priceless. We work on that all summer long."

—Greg Oder, Blue Springs (MO) South High School

"The leadership from our captains and seniors this year was awesome. Developing leaders started years before their senior year. Looking back at old team pictures, our strongest captains were managers as fifth and sixth graders."

—John Schwartz, Mendon (MI) High School

"One thing we did differently this year from other teams in our league and state was our leadership council and character development program."

—Joe Kinnan, Manatee High School (FL)

"We hold a leadership camp in the mountains with our seniors prior to the start of the season. At this camp, we set goals, discuss issues like drugs and alcohol, do problem-solving activities, and help our seniors understand the type of leadership we need to be champions. We feel like it is a great component of our success, and we don't even have a football in camp."

—Don Julian, Sheridan (WY) High School

Develop a system to train your kids to be leaders. Meet on a regular basis to teach them how to be leaders. If you do not do this, how will they become the leaders you want them to be? Leadership does not just happen because they are seniors. It does not just happen because they are an all-league football player two years running. You have to teach leadership; you have to mold leadership. I have covered the way that I have done this through a player committee. In Figure 6-1, you will see the requirements for being on this committee as well as their responsibilities.

Eagles Football 2007 Player Committee

To be on the player committee, a player must:

- Be selected by peers and approved by coaches.
- Have a 3.0 GPA.
- Have a 90 percent attendance rate at weight room workouts.
- Have been a part of this program last season.
- Live a lifestyle consistent with the Christian values that Capistrano Valley Christian teaches.

Player Committee Responsibilities:

- Report to meetings with the head coach and other coaching staff. Meetings will be held every other week during the season and at other needed times.
- Take responsibility of being a leader in the football program.
- Bring to the attention of the head coach and coaching staff any kind of problems, questions, or concerns that the football players might have. Simply be a voice to the head coach.
- Bring to the attention of the players any kind of problems, questions, or concerns that the head coach and other coaching staff might have. Simply be a voice to the players other than the coaching staff.
- Represent the CVCS football program at various events.
- Go above and beyond your peers to represent this football program in the classroom, on campus, on the field, at your church, in the community, etc.
- Help decide on the theme, logo, spirit package clothing, uniform look, and other various ideas that go with a football program.
- Give a player's point of view in regards to discipline issues that might come up.

The coaching staff reserves the right to remove any player from the player committee should they feel the need to do so.

Figure 6-1. Sample player committee guidelines

Bring in Leaders From Your Community to Talk to Your Team

I love to bring in other leaders from my community to come in to address our kids during training camp. I will usually bring in two to four different people to talk to my kids. One of my best years was when I brought in the following leaders: Saddleback College head football coach Mark McElroy, San Clemente High School offensive coordinator and former USC All-American Dave Brown, and one of my best friends, a Marines Corps officer, Captain Kenny Jones. Each man spoke about a different aspect of leadership to my guys.

I have seen this be an effective tool for a few reasons: one, a different perspective from what I'm always talking about; and two, the people I bring are experts in their field, thus giving them authority on leadership that the kids will listen to and respect.

Put Your Leaders in Charge, and Hold Them More Accountable Than the Rest of the Team

> "The one piece of advice I'd give to a head coach wanting to win a state championship is: "As your seniors go, your season goes." Your best players must be your best workers and must be servants within your program."
>
> —Don Julian, Sheridan (WY) High School

In my opinion, one of the absolute best ways to develop leaders is to make them lead. This aspect is especially important in January when your senior leaders are gone from your program. You enter the off-season program with juniors as the oldest kids in the program. They have a choice: to step up as the new leaders, or to stand around and wait for leadership. It is vital to start putting these kids in position to lead right away.

I usually start this process by giving them a simple task, such as creating the new spirit wear package, the shorts, shirts, practice jersey, etc. that we will wear for the next season. This point is also the time to develop the theme for the season. I leave all of this up to my player committee. I give them some guidance on how to make these things happen, I suggest they have a player meeting at lunch in my classroom, and I give them a deadline. It has been really interesting to see how the different groups have handled this. I will tell you one thing; you can usually know how the leadership for the season will go just by how the kids handle this first task.

I have had some groups have two or three meetings to square everything away. They meet to talk about a theme, and get input from the other players on a theme. They present some ideas, and have another meeting or two to solidify everything, and make sure the whole team is on the same page. That is great leadership, and right away these juniors are now stepping up to be leaders. I have given them the authority to step up in to that leadership role, and I have given them the ability to do it.

I have had some other groups just decide everything on their own, in a 20-minute meeting. I have had one group say, "We do not really care, coach. Just choose a theme and the stuff you want us to wear." That team went 0-10, I'm not kidding (the worst season of my life, obviously).

I have always held my captains more responsible than the rest of the team, which is another way to develop leadership. For instance, I put them in charge of setting up the field before practice. They are responsible for getting out our bags, putting the sled bags on, getting the footballs to their right spots, setting up the water, getting cones out of the shed, etc. If the field is not set up by the time we start practice, I hold the leaders accountable. If you talk with my former players, they will tell you that there have been many times when my captains or my player committee started off practice by doing up-downs because the field was not ready to go. Understand that the three or four captains are not the ones setting everything up; they are the ones responsible. This puts them in a position to make things happen, to lead the other players in an everyday task.

What can you put your leaders in charge of to help develop their leadership? It is a very important part of leadership development, and I personally think it is the most important part—putting your kids in leadership positions of everyday tasks. They will either rise to the top as great peer leaders, or they will fail.

Age Doesn't Equal Leadership Ability

One of the greatest student-athlete leaders I've ever had on one of my teams was Phil Wilhelm. He was only a sophomore when he started becoming a fantastic leader. His work ethic in the weight room with our strength coach C.J. Del Balso is what led him to being a great leader. Coach Del Balso came to me during the off-season and said, "You need to think about making Phil a captain." My first thought, because we have been so conditioned as coaches, was, "He is only a sophomore." But Coach Del Balso really challenged this line of thinking. Without a doubt, Phil had all of the qualities we wanted in a captain and leader. His work ethic was second to none, he was the first-to-show-up-and-the-last-to-leave type of kid who overachieved in everything he attempted because of the size of his heart.

We had very poor leadership that year in the junior and senior classes. One reason for that was because there was great leadership in front of them, so those kids were just so used to following that; when they needed to lead, they did not know how. And obviously, I didn't do a good enough job of developing them as leaders. But we had this sophomore class that was pushing our seniors, challenging our seniors. It was great to see. When those sophomores became seniors, we won the league championship. It was a great class of leaders, led by Phil. Do not get caught up in only having seniors as leaders and captains simply because that is the way it has always been. Put kids up as captains who are doing the work, and being great leaders, regardless of their age.

You Must Set the Tone

"My advice to young and upcoming head coaches is to understand leadership is from the top down; just because someone is the head coach does not mean he doesn't have to do the work that he did as an assistant coach. Understand this game is about relationships, too— not just wins and losses."

—Rhett Farmer, Piedmont Academy (GA)

"The one most important aspect of our championship team was leadership and excitement. ...It's your team; take it wherever you want."

—Brent Schroeder, Caledonia (MN) High School

The greatest example of leadership I have ever seen happened in back-to-back years at a church camp up at Bass Lake, California. Two different churches, the same exact campground. The first year, the leader of the trip jumped up on a picnic table with a bullhorn on the last morning, as we were packing up and cleaning up. That person started ordering people around from that bullhorn. "That group there, go pick up the trash on the beach. The group of girls right there, you need to go clean the girl's restroom. Your group there, you guys go clean up the kitchen area."

We had 100 campers up there, 100 teenagers; the place was a disaster by this time of the week. Nobody was doing a thing this "leader" was telling him or her to do. They were standing around talking or playing cards at a table or listening to their walkmans. It took forever for the leaders at that camp to motivate the teenagers to clean up. Why? They were not doing it.

The very next year, with a totally different organization, I am at the same site and the same last morning of camp comes. Again, 100 teenagers and a complete mess.This time, a kindergarten teacher named Cheryl Demus went to the kitchen, grabbed a trash bag and started cleaning up, picking up trash. Next thing you know, teenagers are asking her if she needs help. Next thing you know, seriously, half of the kids are picking up trash, asking for trash bags. The place was spotless in 20 minutes. Somebody starting *doing*.

You have got to lead by example. If you are like the first leader mentioned, do you think that kids will follow you? Or do you think you will get more followers if you are like Cheryl? When you and I played, our coach told us to run through a wall, and we did it. Kids just are not like that anymore. They do not blindly follow you as the head coach. They have to have a reason to do it. Give them a reason. Be the doer; be the leader. You have got to set the tone for leadership by earning the respect of your team. If you walk into the locker room and see trash on the floor, pick it up. If you are just standing around after practice, and balls are lying around, pick them up. This leadership from the top will spread, and you will develop leadership in your kids by this example.

Time-Out

1. Do you have a plan in place to develop leaders? If so, summarize that plan.
2. If you do not have a plan in place to develop leaders, what are three take-aways from this chapter that you can incorporate in to your program to do this?
3. Who are the five top leaders in your football program, and what makes each of them a great leader? Are these five kids teaching others how to become the next great leaders for you?

4. Which of the five tools talked about in this chapter should you incorporate into your program?

5. Coach Greg Oder from Blue Springs South in Missouri said, "This is the first year that I can remember, when we had good strong leadership in every position group. That is priceless. We work on that all summer long." What can your program do this off-season to develop leadership?

7

Team Chemistry: The Most Overlooked Key to Success

Courtesy of Coach Wasson, Southlake Carroll High School (TX)

"Team chemistry was the most important aspect of our championship. We have good team chemistry year in and year out in our program, but this team bonded like no other. When you assemble nearly 100 teenage boys from all walks of life, things are going to happen. Not all players are going to see everything the same way. But this team, during practice and games, was able to put their differences aside for the good of all. Not all people (teams) are willing to do that. Teammates helped each other make good decisions. When poor decisions were made, teammates handled it and worked hard to prevent it from happening again. The poor decision-makers appreciated the effort of their teammates and made great efforts to improve their own decisions. In turn, the effort to improve was noticed by all, which resulted in a unified team. This was most evident by the play of our team in crucial late-game situations. In the end, they were able to put differences or issues aside for the good of the team."

—Bob Godsey, Hartselle (AL) High School

"Not sure what we did differently. However, I know as a staff, we felt we had to take care of us first. We felt that we had the talent and capabilities to be successful; however, we felt strongly that we needed to work hard on team chemistry. By creating a family-like environment and brotherhood amongst the players, we felt strongly that success was possible. Naturally, we would have to make plays as well. However, playing together would certainly optimize those opportunities."

—Ken Lucas, Annapolis Area Christian School (MD)

"Our team-first mentality was really our key this season—the idea that everyone has roles and no matter what your specific roll is it is critical to the team and to the success of the team. This really led to tremendous team chemistry and leadership. We were all in from the student assistants to the players to the staff. It is very hard to articulate, but when that happens, you become a very difficult team for your opponents to deal with."

—Pat Rice, Waunakee (WI) High School

You either have it, or you do not. There really is not a middle ground in the area of team chemistry. When was the last time you heard a coach say, "Our team chemistry is just average." I do not hear that. I have always heard, "Our chemistry needs work" or "Our chemistry is outstanding." I cannot even think what "average" team chemistry would look like.

Chemistry is a scientific word which has to do with how atoms interact with other atoms. I never did very well in my science classes growing up, so it is interesting that I absolutely love studying team chemistry. I firmly believe that building team chemistry is one of the most overlooked aspects of being a head coach. How many times has your own coaching staff discussed building team chemistry around the staff meeting tables? It usually only comes up when things are bad, when kids aren't getting along well together. The coaches who get it in this area can develop a clear advantage over their opponents. By taking the time to develop team chemistry, and getting your "Adams" to interact well with the other "Adams," you can take your team to a place unmatched by your opponents.

Is It Possible to Develop Team Chemistry?

As head coaches, do we really have any control over the chemistry on our football team? Is it possible to develop team chemistry? You only have your kids for a short while during the day, maybe up to three hours. You aren't with them all day, every day. Your season is only one of three seasons during the school year. What about when you lose those kids to other sports? Do we really have control over this aspect of our team?

You absolutely do. You must be proactive in building team chemistry, or it will build itself. The Reagan Administration used a phrase: "If you do not talk about drugs with your kids, somebody else will." And when they ran that commercial, the "somebody else" was a dark shadowy figure in an alley. I really believe in that concept as far as team chemistry is concerned. The Adams are going to interact with the Adams in some way, form, or fashion. Why not spend the time up front, during your training camp or your summer program, to help develop that culture of interaction?

I am always on the lookout for ideas on how to build team chemistry. I am constantly reading books, magazine articles, and online stories about team chemistry. I am fascinated with this topic because I have seen really great teams with great football players have poor chemistry. And vice versa, I have seen teams with very few great football players end up having tremendous team chemistry. For something to be proven scientifically reliable, it must be able to be repeated. I am telling you right now, team chemistry is not as scientific as its name might suggest. Team chemistry is hard to repeat from one year to the next.

I enjoy reading stories about successful businesses because those leaders must develop team chemistry in their offices, or they will fail. Military history is also a great teacher because soldiers must be able to develop chemistry in their teams, or they will fail. Our nation has had some tremendous military leaders to learn from. I encourage you to study team chemistry. Study to find out what makes companies and organizations that you know are doing very well, where people love to work, in order to see what concepts you can take away for your football program.

"They were playing for each other and not themselves. It took a tremendous amount of group mentoring and teaching. We would read any newspaper articles or relative current events that spoke to the team-first mentality. After our second and final loss of the season, a player asked to show a motivational video: How Bad Do You Want It? It turned the season around. We never lost another game. We won nine straight and entered the playoffs as the last seed, and we played every game away, but we never forgot who we were playing for and won a second straight state championship."

—Dan Higgins, Piscataway (NJ) High School

"Team unity and love for each other. Plan for it; practice it daily. It is the single-most influential factor. We preach common purpose, mutual dependence, and shared honor."

—Willie Amendola, Dekaney High School (TX)

"Team chemistry is everything. The 2010 state runner-up had more talent than this year's 2011 championship team did, but they could not all get along. We stressed respect and had several team-building activities."

—Kevin Swift, Gold Beach (OR) High School

Putting Programs in Place to Develop Chemistry

An important aspect of building team chemistry is making sure that you have programs and procedures in place that will naturally help to develop that chemistry. These programs and procedures are some things that happen on a regular basis that are helping your Adams interact with other Adams. An example of a procedure or program I have used in the past is having what we called "home meals."

Every Thursday (the night before the game) when we played at home, we would go to the home of one of the players or coaches for a meal. We asked for parents to host this meal. Many other parents would kick in the funds or the food and drinks to make this happen for us. We would show up 30 minutes after our practice, and have a great meal. This event is always a great night together as a team. Most nights, I would change up the seating assignments. For instance, I would let them all come in and get seated. Then, before our prayer, I would make them mingle by telling everyone to stand and then give them instructions that sophomores had to sit with seniors. The next week, it would be freshmen sit with seniors; maybe it would be only three linemen at a table, or you must have one kid at your table that is brand new this year. I just tried to mix it up like this so that they did not get in to their cliques. This example is just one part of a place in our program that builds team chemistry. Following are some more ideas.

Training Camp Overnighter

I stole this idea right from my high school days. At Fallbrook High School, Coach Tom Pack would arrange trips for us during training camp. There was a time period where we went somewhere every other year for a week of training camp. During my junior year, it was the University of California, Santa Barbara. The following year, we stayed three or four nights in our own gym. This meant we did not have to fundraise every single year for a trip.

I love this idea of getting everyone to stay at the school for two to three nights during Training Camp. Having your kids and coaches sleep on blow-up mats right on campus is just something. I have organized it so that parents come in and take care of all of the food. Kids are responsible for the entertainment and bedding. So, we have had some kids just come in with their sleeping bags and some bring in their mattresses from home. They bring in and set up video games on the big screen, have music, etc. It is a great atmosphere for building chemistry. We are literally on the field or in the gym together for 72 hours straight.

Orientation Groups

I always like to pair my incoming freshman with a senior. I instruct our seniors that they are to be like big brothers to these new kids to campus. I tell them to make sure to check in with their freshmen between every class and at lunch on the first day so that they know where to go, how to find what they need, etc. I also ask our seniors to help mentor and tutor their kids throughout the year. Again, this program helps to create chemistry.

Off-the-Field Fun Nights

I have always been a big believer in getting away from the field as a group. I like to periodically take the entire team to a bowling alley, movie theater, or restaurant in town to help build team chemistry. I think that it is important to do this in season and out of season. Thanks to the advancement of social media, we have seen videos of coaches like Pete Carroll surprise his team with a movie night in the middle of training camp. You see these college kids jumping all around and very giddy when they get a break like this. A few years ago, my team made the section playoffs for the first time in several years. A lot of pressure was on them from all different sources. I wanted to help alleviate that pressure they felt. We were a young team, and I did not want them to crack under it. So, the night before the game, we all went out to dinner and to a mini-golf place together. We did this just to have fun together, and to hopefully take their mind off the game for a few hours, to help them relax.

Swim Party and Skits to Celebrate the End of Training Camp

I have used a great tradition to celebrate the end of training camp. We have a pool party at one of our kids' homes. It is a big barbeque that the parents put together for us. We will have a morning practice, be done by 11 a.m. and head over to a house for a few hours. Again, it's one of those built-in chemistry-builders. The kids really look forward to it, and I have parents knocking down the door to host it.

At this pool party, we will have the underclassmen do skits. We always give them a few days to practice and prepare for these skits. It is always been fun to see them get more and more creative as the years go on. Usually, the skits revolve around making fun of and mimicking the coaching staff and seniors. I do not think we laugh as hard all season long as a team as we do during those couple of hours.

Goal Cards

I stole this idea from Bob Laddoceur at Concord De La Salle. Our staff spent a few days up there a few years ago, and one of the things we really loved was how they do goal cards. The kids come up with three goals per week, and must come with those written on an index card. The three areas are: game goal, practice goal, and lifting goal. At our team meal on Thursday nights, each kid stands up verbalizes his goals, and then chooses a teammate to hold him accountable to those goals during the next week.

For instance, "My game goal is to catch every ball thrown to me, my practice goal is to work on catching for 15 minutes after each practice, and my lifting goal is to do two more reps during my clean max." At the next week's meeting, whomever he chose to hold him accountable will stand up with him and say "Johnny made his game goal, he got all four passes thrown to him, he reached his practice goal by the extra practice each day, but he failed his lifting goal, he was not able to get up the two extra cleans." This one-on-one accountability during the week builds chemistry.

Team Rules Are for the Team

I do not know of anything that destroys team chemistry more than coaches who do not apply the team rules to the team. When the starting quarterback gets preferential treatment, how do you think this makes the third-string quarterback feel? Team chemistry, the Adams getting along with the Adams, will dissolve when they are treated unfairly. If Joe, the fourth-string linebacker, has to do up-downs for being late to practice on Tuesday, and Bill, the starting linebacker is late on Thursday, and gets a pass, then you have a problem. Team rules need to be applied evenly and appropriately.

"This year, our most significant aspect was: believe. Our players believed we were going to be successful this year. Their work ethic was second to none in season and out of season. We were unselfish in the fact that we had no 'I' players, which meant we played as a team the entire season. And lastly was trusting in each other, themselves, and the coaches. You could see that trust in our players' eyes after every play. Each of them knew that they were going to give want ever it took to get the job done along with knowing that the guy next to them was going to do the same thing."

—Jeff Vanleur, Bridgewater/Emery/Ethan High Schools (SD)

"Our team chemistry was great the players had a great drive to finish the deal this season. We worked on being selfless and being team-first mentality. Our motto was: 'If we win, you win.'"

—Maurice Douglass, Trotwood-Madison High School (OH)

"The chemistry that players created among themselves was influenced by our senior leaders. There were no egos to feed, and the players truly believed in each other being accountable for doing their assignments well."

—Bruce Hardin, Providence Day High School (NC)

"I would say the belief in each other we call 'brotherhood.' It helped sustain us through our year-round strength and conditioning program, helped us overcome a week 6 loss in a big game environment, and made the process of building a football program more enjoyable— that and a large group of outstanding young men that are very good athletes that play very good football."

—Scott Bailey, Lamar (MO) High School

"An important aspect of success was our 'one body' philosophy. We stressed all year that there are many parts to a body, and that all are necessary and important. Everyone focused on their role and what they could do to help the entire body be stronger. We stressed that from the very beginning until the championship game."

—John Van Vliet, Lighthouse Christian High School (ID)

"Our team unity was outstanding. It started with our seniors and filtered through all the classes. We have been very blessed over last 30 years, winning the state championship 11 times and playing for the title seven more times. The main ingredient of those teams was unity."

—Barney Hester, Tattnall Square Academy (GA)

"The most important aspect of our state championship season was definitely our team chemistry. Our kids really cared and loved each other."

    —Hal Lamb, Calhoun (GA) High School

"Team unity was the most important part of our state championship season. We try to develop a servanthood type of philosophy. Jesus has given us all a great example of this. Those that are last shall be first. This means that those who serve others will reap the rewards of life."

    —Paul Moro, Blue Ridge High School (AZ)

"The most important aspect of our state championship season was togetherness. Our players have been playing on the same team for several years. Each player has the other's back at all times. This was developed through a sound strength and conditioning program and Fellowship of Christian Athletes. Trust is of the utmost importance."

    —Scott Rials, Elba (AL) High School

"Chemistry that was developed during the off-season and season with our team building activities was the one most important aspect of our championship. Team activities: I take them bowling once a year when we hit a wall with practice. This could be pre-season or in-season. We also do a 'if you really knew me' activity during the pre-season so we can get to know each other better."

    —Mark Del Percio, Middletown (DE) High School

"'Brotherhood is everything' is our constant motto. We believe that by creating relationships between players and players and coaches that a level of trust results that makes teams fight through the tough times. We create tough times during practice where the players have to count on each other. What is learned is that you must be counted on in order to count on others."

    —Rick Streiff, Cathedral High School (IN)

"Team chemistry has been a critical component of every successful team I have coached. Without a "we are all in this together" mentality, teams have a tendency to break apart during the rough parts of a season, and all seasons have rough parts. We attempt to build team chemistry through the off-season. The old saying "Misery loves company" comes into play during our off-season program. We really stress the fact that everyone is working hard to achieve the same goal; everyone is making sacrifices to be good; everyone is paying the same price for success. If we can get that message into our players'

heads, we normally have a very good season. Let's not fool ourselves, though. Talent is the main factor to winning state championships. If your team has talent and the willingness to work as a single unit, success will come."

    —Jeff Gourley, Olathe (KS) South High School

"Without question, the one most important aspect of our team this year was unity. This particular team came together and held each other accountable better than any team I have ever coached. They were unified and extremely cohesive in a way that is hard to describe. 'Stay linked' was our team motto; that undoubtedly was the single-most important reason we were able to win the championship."

    —Jason Herring, Refugio (TX) High School

"This year's team was very unselfish. It did not matter who got the credit as long as our team got the victory. That is a special trait. How did you develop that in your program? I am not sure I did anything differently. This team just listened."

    —Mickey Conn, Grayson High School (GA)

"The most important part of our team this year was the fact that our team was selfless. They were a very close-knit group that didn't care who got the credit, they just wanted to win. You have to find a way to get that through to your athletes. The team will be much better without individuals."

    —Greg Oder, Blue Springs (MO) South High School

"One of the most important ingredients in our program is the emphasis on selflessness. Selflessness is one of our core values and we look to highlight it every chance we can as a coaching staff. Through the course of a high school football season, so many moments of adversity can derail a team. Selflessness, and the togetherness that comes from true selflessness, can carry a team through those moments."

    —Glen McNamee, Central Dauphin High School (PA)

"This wasn't the most talented team that I have had, but it was the best team. These kids liked each other and respected each other and their views. We pushed each other, enjoyed each other, and people were not afraid to laugh or cry with this group."

    —Art Craig, Timberland High School (SC)

Time-Out

1. From your own experience, and what you have read in this chapter, explain why you think Coach Bob Godsey of Alabama's Hartselle High said, "*Team chemistry* was the most important aspect of our championship. We have good team chemistry year in and year out in our program, but this team bonded like no other."
2. Describe the team chemistry from your team this past season.
3. How can you help to develop the team chemistry in your program so that it is better next year than it was this past season?
4. What are three things from this chapter that you plan on implementing right away?
5. What roadblocks are in the way of your Adams getting along wonderfully with the other Adams in your program? What is keeping your program from attaining the best team chemistry possible this next season? What are you going to do about that?

8

Mental Toughness:
Getting the Mind Right

Arrow Santos, Excelsior Charter School (CA)

I have only coached high school football for 13 years. I have been a head coach for eight of those. But I can tell you right now, I learned early on the value of mental toughness. I had a really phenomenal coach when I was a freshman in high school. His name was Coach Greg Madden. He has been coaching at Fallbrook High School for 22 years, starting with my freshman class in 1990. Coach Madden is one of those "manly men." I always thought he was related to *the* Coach Madden, from the Raiders, because they kind of looked alike—both large, imposing men. He has a big barrel chest, stands about 6'3", and has such big hands you can fit a quarter through his wedding ring. Usually, he has a big chaw in one side of his mouth. He is one of those intimidating coaches, until you really get to know the man. Then, you find out he cares more about his players than just about any coach I have had. I called him a few years ago after his wife died. He did not want me to hear him cry, so he changed subjects, and asked what he always asks me, every time I see him now-a-days: "How's your mama doing?"

My very first high school football game was at Temecula High School. I played for the Warriors of Fallbrook High School. Fallbrook and Temecula are bordering towns. It was a big rivalry. The game was at their place, and if you do not know the area, it is in a pretty dry valley and gets very hot in September. I will never forget how hot it was out there at 3:00 p.m. that Thursday when we played.

Coach Madden used to use this drill after stretches when we were already on our backs. It was the last thing we did while stretching. We would have to just hold our legs up in the air, about a foot off the ground, and together. We would dig our hands in to that grass and just hold on for dear life as he would sing a song. "Put 'em up" he would say in that dry, hoarse coaching voice. "Oh Lord, won't you buy me a Mercedes-Benz?" he would go on and sing. It is an old Janis Joplin song. "My friends all drive Porsches/I must make amends/Worked hard all my lifetime/No help from my friends/Oh Lord, won't you buy me a Mercedes-Benz?" Then, he would say the word we couldn't wait to hear: "Down." This meant we could put our legs down. What a relief.

He would go on and on through all of the stanzas of the song. It was grueling. Our hamstrings would be so tight that our backs would tighten up a bit. It was worse during two-a-days, in the morning. It was always a lot harder to hold on to the grass because it would be wet, so that meant it was harder to keep the legs up. The kicker is: if one kid put his legs down, he would say, "All right, put him down. Gotta start over." That would usually start a chorus of groans and yelling at one another. Sometimes, he would have a captain stand up and watch everyone. There were about 65 kids on our team, so inevitably we would have a hard time with having every kid keep his legs up for all of the stanzas of the song. Many times, we would do that drill for 10 to 12 minutes. That's a long time.

A few years later, I was fortunate enough to coach with Coach Madden. It is how I started my coaching career, coaching the freshman team there at Fallbrook High. Now, I could ask him what was up with this drill that seemed to have very little to do with physical conditioning. I was too immature as a freshman to really understand why we were really doing it. Sure enough, my first practice as a coach, I asked Coach Madden why we did this drill.

He laughed. With that big piece of chew tucked in his cheek, he looked at me and said, "You liked that one, didn't you?" He said it with the grin of a Cheshire cat who just swallowed a yellow bird. Then he said, "Mental toughness." I looked at him puzzled. Remember, I was an 18-year-old coach, new to this side of the team. "We did it for mental toughness," he went on to say. "It doesn't have much to do with conditioning the body; it's all about conditioning the mind. How long can you tell your body to keep going when your mind wants to quit?"

It was beginning to make sense. "Chris, listen. Some of the best athletes out on this team, some of the most talented kids, watch them when we do it. Some of those kids are the first to go down. They aren't used to having to fight for something. It's all up here," he told me while pointing to his head.

A light bulb went on in my head. The first lesson about mental toughness, check. It all made sense. The drill made sense. I instantly remembered back to the times when I would be laying on that warm grass, holding my legs up, grasping for grass. And remembering that, yes, my brain would quit before my body. And sometimes when my body would want to quit, my brain would not let it. *What a magnificent drill*, I thought. *What a brilliant coach.*

Remember that game versus Temecula I talked about earlier? We won that game by a very close score, in a hard-fought game. It was one of those games where the first team to quit would lose. It was either 7-6 or 7-0. I cannot remember. I just remember we won our first game as a freshman football team. When we all got together in the end zone, and each coach got to talk to the team, Coach Madden started his talk out with, "Oh Lord, won't you buy me a Mercedes-Benz?" And we all started yelling and cheering. We went nuts. Then he said, "Was it worth it?" We all yelled, "Yes!" We sang songs all the way back to school on that old yellow bus. I'll never forget that trip. We thought we were the greatest team on the planet.

That was my indoctrination in to mental toughness, and its importance in the game of football. Taught to me by a great man, a veteran coach with a passion to help develop kids. I'll never forget the lessons of Coach Madden. He is still coaching at Fallbrook High; last year, he was honored at halftime of the homecoming game, he was the grand marshall.

Mental toughness came back as one of the top 10 characteristics of a championship-caliber program through this research I did. Many coaches pointed to the fact that you must condition the mind just as much as the body. I know that many coaches do not have this type of training or background. The psychological side to the game of football, which I learned a lot about during my sports psychology classes from one of the best (Vance Tammen at Concordia University in Irvine) is an area in which coaches should receive training and help. It was the most valuable part of my experience while earning my master's degree in athletic administration. He helped to totally change the way I approach my team. I am glad I took his course because, just one year later, we won a league championship. And I'm telling you right now, without this course, and my new understanding of sports psychology, I do not know that I would have been able to teach my kids about mental toughness the way I did.

During the summer of 2010, I know we had a pretty decent football team coming back. We had some of our key players back as seniors, and were primed for a great season. I thought we had a chance to battle for the league championship *if* everything went our way, and we stayed healthy and got some lucky bounces.

A team named Avalon was in our league, and they were *seven*-time league champions, *seven* years in a row. Big, strong kids from the island of Catalina off the coast of Southern California; I was coaching in Orange County at the time, a little school called Capistrano Valley Christian. Their enrollment had taken a huge hit due to many factors, and we were left playing eight-man football. There were 17 kids in my program: nine freshmen, two sophomores, and six seniors. Freshmen are pretty useless on a varsity football field playing against 17- and 18-year-old young men, even if it is eight-man football. But we were fortunate enough to have a couple of them who started. We basically had 10 "varsity" players.

We would still have my Jimmys on the field playing their Joes. It always comes down to that. And I knew that my Jimmys were intimidated by those big, strong kids. They *pounded* us 55-8 in 2009. That tells you about their team right there. We were a .500 team that year, too, qualified for the playoffs. It's not like we were 0-10.

I had a lot to do with the mental aspect of our guys for this upcoming season. I *had* to convince them we could beat this team. So, that summer I started to read a lot of books and writings from coaches and psychologists regarding mental toughness. "That is where we will win this game," I thought to myself one day in the office, "with mental toughness."

So, I started soaking it up, and reading everything I could, to prepare my boys for mental toughness, because I knew that if I did my job convincing these boys to be tough in their minds, they could beat Avalon, even at their place.

I came across a *fantastic* definition of mental toughness, and I started preaching it to my kids a few weeks before Avalon. I wanted to plant the seed in their minds, that we must become more mentally tough than we were. Remember when I said we had six seniors? Going in to the Avalon game, we only had four. We had lost two two-way starters—both seniors—to broken legs leading up to that game. Our kids had every reason in the book to fold losing those two studs.

In their book *What Is This Thing Called Mental Toughness? An Investigation of Elite Sports Performers*, Graham Jones, Sheldon Hanton, and Declan Connaughton of the United Kingdom interviewed elite athletes as well as elite-level coaches and sport psychologists, and developed the following definition of mental toughness:

"Having the natural or developed psychological edge that enables you to: generally, cope better than your opponents with the many demands (competition, training, lifestyle) that sport places on a performer; specifically, be more consistent and better than your opponents in remaining determined, focused, confident, and in control under pressure."

When I read this definition, I absolutely loved it. In fact, I put it up on the board in our video room for the kids to see several weeks in a row. I thought to myself, "That's it. This is what we need to beat Avalon." A few things stood out to me from this definition:

- "… cope better than your opponents …"
- "… be more consistent and better than your opponents in remaining determined, focused and confident while under pressure."

There was no doubt that this league championship football game would be a tough one. We would have to keep it close in order to win the game. I had to get my kids to believe we could win the game. I had to get them practicing this idea of "coping better" and responding to pressure better. So, we put more pressure on them in practice. Some of the weeks that year, we knew that our practices would be harder mentally and physically than the games. That is just the kind of season we had. We had to manufacture a lot of adversity in practice. I thought our coaching staff did great at that.

I will never, ever forget having breakfast at a little cafe on the island the morning of the game. A patron whom I did not know came up as he was leaving and said "Coach, good luck today. Is your varsity team playing out here today, too?" He assumed we were the JV team. That should tell you right there how small we were, and what the folks in town thought of our little team. And he was not being a smart aleck; he was dead serious. One reason that man thought that we were the JV team was because we only had 11 players. Avalon suited up 24 that day. That's right, our 11 versus their 24—almost a modern-day David-and-Goliath story.

We get out to the field that day; it was a cloudy and misty October morning, and I could tell right away that the Avalon kids were not mentally prepared and focused. Sure, it was an hour, maybe an hour and 15 minutes before the game, but I had seen a lot of football teams prepare, and I knew these guys were not nearly as prepared as our team was. I saw in our boys' eyes as we walked the field that they were focused and ready to play, and I saw that Avalon was looking past us.

It was a tough game. It was a back-and-forth game, and one of the most stressful of my career. Why? We were simply outmanned, and I knew it. We gave up 40 pounds per player on average. We had three freshmen starting on the offensive side of the ball. Three. We were playing for a league championship, the first at our school in eight years. Both teams were 2-0 in league, and I just knew that with the remaining games on the schedule, this game would determine the league championship. It was stressful because we were mainly a running team, but we knew coming into this game that we must throw the ball to win. And the weather didn't make that easy on us. (We eventually threw for more yards than we rushed for the first time in five years.)

At halftime, we were down by two points, 22-20. Avalon usually got better as the game went on, so there was cause for concern. I did not want our kids folding up their tents and packing for home, because traditionally at this school, that was their reputation. They did not like to fight for much when the going got tough, they just weren't that mentally tough.

Well, we come out to start the second half and on our first drive, we give up a safety, and Avalon has all of the momentum. Would our kids fold now? We were down 24-20 at about the midway point through the third quarter.

We scored toward the later part of the third quarter on a long pass by our freshman quarterback to another freshman playing. That put us up for the first time in the game, 26-24. We opted to go for two because we didn't want to kick in the rainy conditions. We missed the two-point conversion which left us beatable with only a field goal, but I knew they wouldn't be able to kick that in the wet, rainy conditions. That was the final score, 26-24. With about one minute and 30 seconds left, they were able to put together a drive. But we forced a fumble on about our own 20-yard line, took over, and put together a drive of our own to run out the clock.

Mental toughness was our MVP that day. It won this game, and this game won the league championship. We went on to beat our next two opponents soundly. That game was a real test for our kids in the area of mental toughness. The mental toughness training for that game started in the summer, with a coach trying to learn more about how to instill it in his kids. I firmly believe that without the mental toughness training that we went through, we would not have had the ability to win that game out on the island.

Three Keys to Teaching Mental Toughness

Define It for the Kids, and Continually Bring Them Back to It

"We spent a great deal of time on the mind-set each week. Mental toughness—it's not the what, but the how. Mental toughness is being able to go from play to play, stay in the moment, and being able to focus. Being excellent is the ability to do common things with uncommon discipline and enthusiasm. Don't get caught up in distractions that have nothing to do with the moment/play/game, etc. This takes mental toughness, which is a learned behavior.

"This takes tremendous mental and physical condition. Therefore, these are things we can control, and don't focus on the things you have no control over. Being mentality tough requires the ability to overcome adversity. You will not get there without conquering the

adversity—and that's the toughest part. And this team chose to do just that. Always put the emphasis on the team."

—Hal Wasson, Southlake Carroll High School (TX)

Early in this chapter, I shared a great definition of mental toughness. We cannot just tell kids to be mentally tough; we have to define that and teach what it means. If you fail to find a definition for your team, you cannot just expect kids to just be mentally tough. It is your job as the head coach to set that tone and set the expectation. I suggest bringing them back to this definition of mental toughness on a weekly basis in a few different areas: the film room, the meeting room, on the field as a group, and one-on-one with kids. Everyone learns differently, each of those kids is going to pick up different parts of the mental toughness definition you are trying to get your team to buy in to at different times.

"We always like to challenge our kids, and we had a special challenge for them this year. Our senior class is a very talented class that had essentially underachieved. This was their challenge: to prove they were more than just a group of talented individuals. They were challenged to prove they were also mentally and physically tough. The previous season they had demonstrated the inability to deal with in-game adversity, and so we focused on developing that mental toughness and trust in one another."

—Mike Boyd, Nouvel Catholic Central High School (MI)

"I believe the biggest task of a head coach in high school athletics is creating a mindset and an expectation in your players. You have to get them to believe that they are doing it better and working harder than anyone else. If you get a kid coached up well, there is a high likelihood he will be successful, but if you get a passionate kid coached up well, he is unstoppable. A state championship season is a very long haul; the kids have to want to be back at practice on Monday for the 16th week of the season; if they don't, it will come out in their play."

—Jon Ellinghouse, Sierra Canyon High School (CA)

You've Got to Practice and Teach It on the Field All Year Long—It Does Not Just Happen Overnight

"It is just as important to develop players' mental toughness and 'heart power' as it is to develop physical talents and skills. In crucial moments, these often are more important in the determination of success and failure than physical attributes. Also, do not be afraid of letting kids sit and talk about lofty goals as long as you reinforce that such goals can only be achieved through dedication, hard work, and taking things one workout, one practice, one game at a time."

—Joe Harbour, Norwayne High School (OH)

Kids are not asked to be tough anymore, physically or mentally. We have to take that on ourselves, as their coaches, leaders, and mentors. I hear football coaches yell things from the sidelines like "Be strong," "Be tough," and "Don't give up." But that stuff cannot just happen overnight. You've got to work at developing mental toughness throughout the year.

One of the best ways to do this in the off-season strength and conditioning portion of your program is by pushing your kids to succeed and reach their goals. Do not just open the weight room and think you are doing a good job because you have some kids getting stronger. Have the kids make goals for themselves in different categories in the off-season. Goals for the different lifts you do, for their speed and agility on the field. Continuously talk about these goals, and post these goals. This will help your kids to develop a mentality of toughness as they strive to beat themselves. If they fail to meet their goals, hold them accountable. Make them better. Push them to new heights in the off-season. Stretch their minds by stretching their goals beyond what they think they can do.

"I think our kids are very poised and show a lot of mental toughness. We focus on that in everything we do throughout the year."

—Hank Carter, Lake Travis High School (TX)

"We have been to the state championship six of the last seven years, winning four titles. We are the third-smallest public school in a conference of 14. The thing I believe we do differently than other schools in our league is that we don't focus on the negatives, but concentrate on our positive. We could sit back and complain that we are a small school and we are playing schools with 1,000 more students than us. Instead, we use that as a positive. We tell our student-athletes we must work harder than other schools in order to be successful—and this starts in the weight room. We want our student-athletes to do all sports, and our coaches at our school agree and encourage their athletes go out for other activities. This is what sets our school apart from the others, in a time of traveling teams and specialization of sports: we are unified as coaches. We find, because of this, our kids are great competitors, and we win a lot of games in pressure situations—because they compete year-round. They have learned how to compete and play hard."

—Pat Murphy, Capital High School (MT)

"We were always able to respond to adversity, no matter what happened our kids responded like champions. I believe that our coaching staff taught our players how to respond to pressure and how to respond to those situations. We always talk about handling what we can control and doing that in a positive manner."

—Seth Stinton, Melissa (TX) High School

Coach Stinton brings up a great point: teaching players how to respond to pressure and how to respond to those situations. How do you do this on the field during the week? If you are not putting your kids in pressure situations during the week, do not expect them to just turn that on Friday night.

Teach Your Kids to Be Confident by Putting Them in Position to Succeed

Confidence breeds confidence, which breeds more confidence. I believe confidence is a real key to mental toughness. Put your kids in pressure situations during the week. I love doing this. For one, it usually gets the intensity up at practice. Secondly, it changes up the monotony of practice. And third, it helps to prepare them mentally. One way I've done this in the past is with a surprise team red zone time. Right after our dynamic warm-up, instead of going in to special teams or tackling, what we usually do, we will send everyone to the sidelines, and then get our first-team offense out on the 10-yard line. Defensive staff gets a scout team defense out there, and we get after it, right out of the shoot.

The kids are usually a little dazed when this happen. It is out of the practice routine. Sometimes, they just are not mentally ready for it, because they have not physically and mentally prepared for it. But you have got to be able to adapt and overcome mentally to sudden change during a football game. Coaches, if you are not teaching this, they will not do it.

We will tell them they have three downs to get the ball in, or they lose. They have to do up-downs or a few cross-fields or something. There has to be some sort of incentive there for them to win. We put the pressure on them during this time, trying to put them in a position to succeed, so they know what it is like to succeed when they are not ready for a sudden change mentally. Do something to throw your kids for a loop, a big sudden change in your practice, and see how they respond. I believe that the key is: you must get them to where they have success doing this both mentally and physically. Do not allow it to get negative, or when that sudden change comes Friday night, it will be negative. You want them to have the confidence that they have "been there, done that."

> "Gold Beach High School has played in five state titles games in the last seven years, winning two and losing three. Our kids and community are committed to outworking all of our opponents in league and in the state. Investing more, therefore, we play more determined to win, rather than hoping to win. Also, we returned to a true option quarterback, rather than a great quarterback, but not necessarily an option quarterback."
>
> —Kevin Swift, Gold Beach (OR) High School

> "Dedication to the team goal or mission and complete true belief that it can indeed be reached was the most important aspect of our championship. Intense off-season training and character building reinforced our sense of commitment as well as helped us develop

a 'no doubts' mentality that as long as we fight together as a team, there are no limits to what we can do. This was displayed no more clearly than in the state finals game, when we fell behind for the very first time in the game late in the fourth quarter in a manner that could have broken the spirit of many teams. Our senior quarterback walked into the huddle, simply said, "No doubts, we got this,' and then we marched down the field to score the game winning touchdown with 30 seconds left in the game."

—Joe Harbour, Norwayne High School (OH)

"I think the most important characteristic of our team this year was resiliency. For us, that started with tremendous leadership from our senior class. We were not the most physically talented team in the state, but we played extremely hard, we played very smart, and we played very unselfishly together. In the playoffs, we were behind twice by three scores at the half, yet kept our poise and found a way to win the game. Our coaches and players were resilient, never panicked, and believed in each other no matter what we encountered. It takes talent to win a championship, but a lot of very talented teams never come close because they lack some of the characteristics I just mentioned. This was a very special team, one that both our school and community are very proud of and won't soon be forgotten."

—Kevin Wright, Carmel (IN) High School

Time-Out

1. Was your team this past season mentally tough? Why or why not? What are some examples of that mental toughness?
2. What does your program do to teach mental toughness?
3. What are two things you are going to implement in your program from this chapter on mental toughness?
4. Hal Wasson of Southlake Carroll in Texas said, "Being mentality tough requires the ability to overcome adversity. You will not get there without conquering the adversity—and that's the toughest part." How is your staff teaching your players to overcome adversity?
5. Who can you reach out to on your campus or in your community to help your staff and players to get training on becoming more mentally tough as a program?

9

Preparation: Leave No Stone Unturned

Brian Thompson, Logan (UT) High School

"There are no shortcuts. There is not a magic bullet that cures everything. You just need to grind—in season, off-season—in so many different areas, all of which are key to the success of your program. We try never to be satisfied and take things for granted; we are always looking to improve and get better. The other thought may sound cliché, but worry about the game in front of you. We really try to stay in the moment and understand what we need to do that week to be successful. We believe that if we have a great week in terms of preparation, this will show on Friday nights."

—Pat Rice, Waunakee (WI) High School

Championship-caliber football programs know how to prepare their kids to be successful on Friday nights. Preparation is one of the most important aspects of any great organization, and it is no different for a high school football team. An old adage says: "Failure to prepare is preparation for failure." That is true. The great leaders—and coaches—separate themselves from the pack when they learn to prepare their troops in such a way that no stone is left unturned. Friday nights cannot be a laboratory, where you experiment; they should be a surgeon's table, where you execute.

"My best advice would be the same advice I would give to a first-year head coach, and that would be the only thing guaranteed concerning your next football season is that you are going to have adversity. So plan for it, and understand that your ultimate success is going to depend on how you deal with whatever adversity comes your way. Championship teams always seem to find a way to overcome obstacles. That is why at each end of our locker room we have a sign that reads: 'No Excuses: Win the Day.'"

—Kevin Wright, Carmel (IN) High School

"Be well prepared, and have a sound plan. You must have more than one plan in case things don't go as well as you hope for. Keep your plan simple so adjustments can be made at any time."

—Scott Rials, Elba (AL) High School

Practice Makes Perfect

"This year, as a staff, we were better at practice planning and time allocation for all of our practices. We went to a clinic at Boise State, and it really opened our eyes on how to break away from a traditional football practice. Specifically, we tried not to have a period go over 8 to 10 minutes max. This allowed us to make sure we could rep more technique daily. At our level, we don't always have the prototypical

kids in positions, so technique was absolutely huge for us. Great technique gave the kids added confidence against bigger/stronger opponents. We also tried to have at least three sessions in practice where we divided them up and held different types of contests where there was a clear winner and a clear loser, some contests that didn't have anything to do with football. Reinforcing how to win."

    —Jeff Lindsley, Grangeville (ID) High School

I have never seen Boise State practice, but after reading this quote, now I want to. Football practices have evolved over the years. From the Bear Bryant days of three-hour-long practices with an hour and a half of team time to shorter, crisper, music blasting atmospheres. Part of the reason these practice differences exist is due to rule changes at the college level. Another part of the differences is due to the fast-paced, no-huddle offenses that are abundant these days. You have to practice like that if you want to play like that. But I also think that the changes we are seeing with practices are because our society has changed. Attention spans are shorter now than they were when most of you coaches played. Kids get bored, and we have to capture their attention. Following are three keys to having great practices: be organized, be prepared, and be enthusiastic.

Be Organized

Some coaches are very organized, and some are not. For some, the idea of having a minute-by-minute practice plan in the hands of every coach is a no-brainer, and for some it is a foreign idea. I firmly believe that in order to get the most out of every single practice, you have got to sit down and plan out those practices minute by minute. This should be done with your coordinators so that you get their input and buy-in for the practice schedules. I had a great mentor in Perry Krosschell, who had just come from the college level while we worked together at Linfield Christian in Temecula. He was the head coach there for a few years, and groomed me to take his spot when he moved to Iowa to start a football program at Unity Christian in Orange City, Iowa.

Coach Krosschell introduced me to the minute-by-minute practice plan idea, and I've used it ever since (Figure 9-1). From your pre-practice time to your post-practice time, everything should be planned out and put on paper and in the hands of your coaches so they know exactly what to expect and when to expect it. Nothing is worse on the practice field than starting a new drill, only to be called over by the head coach for team time. This will not happen if your coaches are organized by the practice schedule they should have ahead of time. For training camp, I would give all of our practice schedules to our coaches before the first practice. They would get two weeks of practices that myself and the coordinators would have put together during June and July. Obviously, some of these will adjust as you get going, but with putting them on spreadsheets, they become very easy to make last-minute adjustments.

Period	Time	Tue PM—Offense
1	230	Warm
2	235	Warm
3	240	Punt
4	245	Kickoff
5	250	Kick return
6	255	Two-point plays
7	300	Team offense
8	305	Team offense
9	310	Team offense
10	315	Team offense
11	320	Team offense
12	325	Defensive set recognition
13	330	Defensive set recognition
14	335	Defensive set recognition
15	340	Tackling
16	345	Tackling
17	350	Conditioning
18	355	Conditioning
19	400	Cool-down
20	405	Touch-up

Figure 9-1. Sample minute-by-minute practice plan

I also try to get these in the hands of the players, so they know what to expect. At the very least, I would post it in the locker room before each practice so they could get a sense of what we were trying to do that day.

Be Prepared

One of the biggest practice time-wasters is when coaches say "Okay, offensive line over this way. Now, go get me those bags in the shed." All of a sudden, he is losing four minutes of his 20-minute individual time because he was not prepared. Prepared coaches need to set their drills up before practice begins. This step is key to getting the most out of your practice time together. Get your bags, cones, balls, and sleds prepared ahead of time. Use your kids to help do this if you are not fortunate enough to have managers. Get your gear to the sidelines nearest to where you will be so that you are ready to go as soon as your time starts. This approach will help you make the most out of every single snap.

Using a script is a key to an effective practice. If you fail to put together a script for both your offensive and defensive team time, you really are shooting in the dark with what needs to be done. Again, your coordinators should put these scripts together, and they should be on the practice plan so that everyone is on the same page, and you can move through things quickly.

Also, this plan will help you avoid doing some plays too many times, and some plays not enough. Have your play list right there with you as you put your practice scripts together. Another thing this script will do is give your plays numbers. What is more frustrating as an assistant coach? Say you are the running backs coach, and you are teaching a kid off to the side, and you do not hear the play called. So, there goes the offense to the line of scrimmage, and they run a play, and you have no idea what you are looking for. As the head coach, once we got off the script, I would always yell out the play number a few times so that my coaches knew what we were doing. These aspects are all a part of being prepared.

Be Enthusiastic

Enthusiasm is key to getting the most out of your players *and* coaches. It is the biggest challenge for me, to be honest. I am not naturally enthusiastic as some guys are. I am more of a pessimist than an optimist—more of an "all business, all the time" type of guy. I have had to work at being enthusiastic as the head coach. Face it, if you are not leading from the front with enthusiasm, you better either get some great assistants who are doing this, or find a way to "fake it until you feel it." Steve Chamberlin, a former coach on my staff, taught me how to do this. He was always enthusiastic and positive. One of those coaches who really pumps kids up daily because of his attitude. He was always encouraging me to find positive things and "fake it until you feel it." I really think that is great advice.

If you are not being enthusiastic, are kids going to be excited about playing in your program? Are they (and your coaches, for that matter) going to enjoy coming to practice? I believe they need to enjoy it to a certain extent in order for you to maximize your time with them. Enthusiasm on the practice field spreads like wildfire. Jump around a little bit, and yell positive things. See what this does for your kids. If you are not naturally an enthusiastic person, they will love to see it, and you will bring a new energy to the practice field.

Find kids to praise, find kids to pump up, find kids to high-five, and find kids to encourage. So many times, as coaches, we are correcting and teaching and training. Imagine if your boss never gave you praise, never gave you some enthusiastic "atta boys." (For some of you, this example isn't hard to imagine, is it?) Remember what it was like as a player. The grind of practice can be hard. Be enthusiastic in your praise of the kids' efforts and attitudes (if they are deserved, that is), and it will make practice much more enjoyable for your kids. Whether or not you agree with this idea that it's got to be enjoyable, look for some ways to notch up the enthusiasm next season.

The Film Room

"We lift and practice during the off-season, we have excellent talent, and as a staff we put in hours watching film and preparing for our opponents."

—Greg Maccarone, Glassboro (NJ) High School

I will never forget watching film in my classroom in 2002 (I was at Linfield Christian as a varsity assistant) when I found a telltale sign while watching the foot of a quarterback at Calvary Murrieta, our biggest rival. I noticed that when his right foot was flat, they were running the ball. When he was up on the ball of that right foot, heel off the ground, he was dropping back to pass. You should have seen him during the game. He was freaking out because our noseguard was yelling out "Pass, pass, pass" or "Run, run, run." Then, the backers would shout it out. They had no clue how we knew. We beat them 35-0. Film is essential for a championship-caliber football program.

If you have been around for a while, you know that watching film has come a *long* way since you and I were in school. Now, I am not that old so I do not remember the reel-to-reel sessions I remember my coaches in high school telling me about. But I do remember making highlight films by meticulously watching game film, and writing down the play time of an outstanding play. Then, I would sit there for hours on end, doing the VHS-to-VHS recording. Do you remember those days? Now, you have programs like Hudl® and Landro®, where you can instantly pull up all of the highlights from the last season in seconds.

I have always believed using film to prepare your players is of utmost importance. I have always used it to both prepare and correct my players. My freshman football coach, Scott Carpenter, used to always say, "The eye in the sky don't lie," and he is right. I am not sure who gets credit for saying that first, but whoever it was is a genius: the eye in the sky never lies. Nothing is better for teaching your players than the use of real game and practice film.

Way to Use Film to Prepare Your Players— Be B.R.I.E.F.

B—brevity. We must remember that these players have short attention spans. Heck, some of our coaches have short attention spans. Watching film for hours on end will do no good for most of the kids these days. We live in an "instant society," where patience is a thing of the past. Err on the side of having short film sessions rather than long ones. This approach will keep your kids tuned in to what you are trying to convey. I have seen or heard of teams watching film for an hour and a half at a time; that's a full length feature film. I do not believe that you will be effective if using this method.

R—ready. Be prepared before you hit the film room. Make sure your coaches are prepared before they hit the film room. You ask your players to be prepared, so make sure you are. Nothing is worse for players than to sit in that film room and watching coaches try to figure out what to watch, how much of it to watch, etc. You will spend unneeded time in the room if you fail to prepare.

What I did with my staff was, when we broke down the offense, for instance, the rookie coach in the room would have a piece of paper with him, and the line coach and I would tell him, "Play 5, Phil needs to fix his stance here; Joey needs to cut his route much earlier than he did." That coach would then write out those words exactly, and we would go through the film with this paper with us. This approach helped us get through the film in a timely manner.

I—inquire. Ask your kids questions. Get them thinking. Do not just talk and talk and talk and talk. Remember, kids are only going to listen if they want to. And they are not going to want to listen if they are just there for a lecture, and butt chewing. You and I would sit through it, and we would listen. For the most part, most kids today will tune you out. Do not just tell them they ran a poor route; ask why they didn't do what they practiced all week. Do not just tell them they lined up in the wrong formation; ask how it was communicated in the huddle, and where the error was. When I really started asking questions during film, one thing I learned was that our team communication had to improve. And that was from the top down. Asking your players questions, inquiring of them will create active listeners, which you want in your film sessions.

E—encourage. You've got to make sure to point out the good in your film sessions, too. As coaches, usually we have the tendency to just teach, chew out, challenge, and question the kids in film. Remember that our job as coaches is more than just what happens between the lines. Think back to your film sessions as a player. Do you remember when one of your coaches pointed out a dynamite play, a fantastic block, supreme effort? How did that make you feel?

Find some plays to encourage your kids. Remember, even the stars need a pat on the back and positive confirmation of what they are doing. Make sure to notate some great things you see as you break things down with your coaches. Take time to enjoy that success in the film room, and to encourage your players. I believe it will come back tenfold to you. Their desire to please you will improve; their effort will improve if you are encouraging them during film time.

F—facts. "Just the facts, ma'am." Remember this old detective saying from *Dragnet*? I don't know about you, but I know I have had some Saturday mornings where I went into the film session in a pissed-off mood because of our loss, and I was going to "let the kids have it." How many of you or your coaches used a phrase like "wait until films" after your Friday night loss? I am sure the kids are just thrilled with the expectation of showing up to films with you. Do not use your film room time to get emotional with your kids. Yes, it is an emotional game, and those emotions will come roaring back after a loss when you press play. However, remember that you are the mature adult professional. Keep your cool, Coach. It is not easy. Not by any means. This stage is where the accountability with your coaches will help. Stay to the facts of what you need to teach your kids through the film. The reason you are watching it is to get better as a football team, not to make yourself feel better by yelling at your kids, or letting your emotions get the best of you. Stick to the X's and O's, just the facts.

Preparing Your X's and O's

"Find an offensive and defensive system that you are comfortable with, and stay with it. We have run an I formation option offense and a 52 (3-4) defense for 30 years. Our kids know and understand the system. Another thing that makes a difference is playing as many players as you can whether as starters on offense or defense, or as starters on a special team."

—Barney Hester, Tattnall Square Academy (GA)

Preparing your kids to execute starts on the practice field, and continues in the film room, but the bedrock of it all is your philosophy of how to both move and stop the ball. This book is not about X's and O's; countless books and films are available about the "how-to," regarding the three phases of the game. However, coaches did give credit to their offensive and defensive systems for their championships. What you are going to run offensively and defensively is a crucial part of a championship-caliber football program. Preparing your team to run a certain offense, defense, and special teams is key to having success.

"If I, as the head coach, have done anything successfully, one thing is to coach to your strengths. I have never been totally sold on one system that we insist on kids fitting that system. The talents of our kids dictate what our offensive and defensive philosophy is for that group of kids. It does change from one class of kids to another and from decade to decade."

—Matt Lindsay, Bishop Luers High School (IN)

"I'm not sure what we do differently. I just know that we try to stay at the cutting edge of offensive, defensive, and strength and conditioning knowledge each year to make sure we put our kids in the best possible positions in order to succeed. I think our visits to colleges in the spring have been a tremendous help."

—Hank Carter, Lake Travis High School (TX)

"We were balanced on offense. We could beat you running the ball or throwing the ball. We could take what you gave us and beat you with it.

"Defensively, our team was well-coached, and they played like an 11-piece machine. Team-wise, we went off during the first week of two-a-days and had camp at Wayland Baptist. We became like a family, as in everyone valued the team above themselves. We became family; as coaches, the players allowed us to enjoy them. They followed our lead, and then they led the same direction. It was special. It went far beyond the players; the parents were just as bought in as anyone."

—Greg McClendon, Midland (TX) Christian High School

"On offense, we implemented the pistol to our flex bone, and it gave us the ability to spread the field and allowed our quarterback (5'6"/160 lbs) a chance to make the plays in the crunch when we had to. We allowed our players the ability to make the plays when they had to; we were not that far off from winning the state the past few years (51-4 the past four years). We decided as a team that, to beat us, you would have to beat the whole team, and the one game we lost this year brought us closer together. We didn't blame players or coaches; we all took responsibility."

—Art Craig, Timberland High School (SC)

"The coaches taught on the field each day and kept practices well-organized. Watching film and making the daily improvements was a big help in the stretch run of the playoffs. Our quarterback managed the games well, and the defense was productive in getting the ball to our offense with good field position. Blocking punts, field goals, returning punts, and kickoffs were a big part of our game plan and were executed by the players."

—Bruce Hardin, Providence Day High School (NC)

"We make sure we play all three aspects of the game: offense, defense, and special teams. Our special teams play this year was outstanding. We had three successful fake punts, a punt return for a touchdown, and a kick of return for a touchdown. Use special teams to change momentum."

—Travis Cote, Bishop Guertin High School (NH)

"We run the spread no-huddle offense. This seems to be a big plus for us because it allows us to put pressure on the defense. We use our same personnel with different formations. The no-huddle gives us an advantage in that we can dictate tempo."

—Scott Rials, Elba (AL) High School

"This year, we ran a speed-up no-huddle offense and let our quarterback call 95 percent of the plays from scrimmage. This gave us a tremendous advantage on the field. We ran that offense in practice and could get in 60 to 80 plays in a 25-minute offensive segment. It not only made practice upbeat and fun, but it was great conditioning."

—Ray Steele, Indian River High School (DE)

"One thing that we do differently compared to other teams is that we focus on ourselves more than our opponent. We run the same six or seven plays out of our base set every year. In an era when everyone is changing offenses every year, we have been able to continue our success in the execution of our plays because of a commitment to our offense long term."

—Rhett Farmer, Piedmont Academy (GA)

"Less is more. Some guys have play cards that look like a cheap family restaurant menu. We have eight running plays, two play-action passes, and five three-step passes. Find what you believe in, and get good at it."

—John Ivlow, Bolingbrook (IL) High School

"We spread the field with talented receivers and made the defense defend 53 yards wide by 50 yards deep. By spreading the field, we make the defenders play in space. Pass protection must be flexible enough either through blocking scheme or by route break-off to keep the defense off your quarterback."

—Bruce Kozerski, Holy Cross High School (KY)

"We were able to maximize our potential weekly by utilizing a game plan and skill sets of the players to attack against the weakness of the opposing team. We would run more if they had trouble with the run game, we would tweak the defense to add more or less to the box to defend and attack what they did well, and we always used special teams to help dictate field position."

—Dan Higgins, Piscataway (NJ) High School

"We try to run an offense and defense that is unique to the Canistota Hawks. Running a unique offense and defense makes other teams have to prepare for us instead of defending just another I formation team or 4-3 defense. We run an option-based offense, where our players all have specific roles to play. Each player has to perform as if he has the ball or the play is coming to him. Defensively, each player has a lane to fill."

—Lenny Schroeder, Canistota (SD) High School

"We have created an offensive system that has the ability to drive the football consistently in league play and is not dependent on the big play. We are capable of the big play, but we were able to win games without it. Defensively, we were able to limit the big-play production of our opponents and force them to grind out drives, which very few were capable of doing on a consistent basis. Special teams-wise, we do focus on creating the big play; we had nine touchdowns on special teams this past year."

—Joe Prud'homme, Nolan Catholic High School (TX)

"Our school is an incredible story of success. At one point before I arrived, Gretna had lost 44 consecutive games, and now has won five of the past nine state championships. I took over in 2010 after Gretna had won back-to-back states. We have won these state championships with three different head coaches. When I took over, I had a reputation of taking over terrible programs and turning them into winners, so when I took this job, people expected us to be rebuilding, but all we have done in my three years is play in two state championships, winning one. Our football program currently holds the state's longest streak of winning 10 or more games for nine consecutive years.

"The first key for me and our kids is that we are a spread team. I was a wing-T guy until I showed up, but I am not stupid. They weren't broke, so no need to fix it. So we stayed in the spread and rest is history.

"I am a defensive guy, so the biggest key was us changing what we did on defense. I changed them from a 3 stack to a 40 with four linebackers, sometimes only two, so more of a 4-2. This year, we never gave up more than two touchdowns in any game, and even in the blowouts our second team was tremendous."

—Kevin Saunders, Gretna High School (VA)

"Don't get too fancy with the offense and defense. It's like the KISS method: keep it simple, stupid. Some coaches want to run 10 different offenses and defenses, and the kids are so confused they can't execute anything."

—Larry Glatczak, Centralia/Wetmore (KS)

Time-Out

1. What are three areas of your program that can be strengthened in this area of preparation?
2. What would your players say about the structure of your practices? Do you plan every single minute of it, to see that not one minute is wasted?

3. How has your film time improved over the last five years because of technology? Think back to how you did things five years ago; is your preparation better now? How or how not?

4. Does your staff do their best possible job of preparing your players with the X's and O's? What changes do you need to make so that your kids can be even more prepared next season?

5. Which quote did you like the most from this chapter, and why? What are you going to apply from that quote to your program's preparation?

10

Building Trust and Confidence

Brian Thompson, Logan (UT) High School

"If you want to win a state championship, you have to get the players bought into 'you' as much as the program. They have to be willing to sacrifice themselves for the success of the team. They have to believe and honor the fact that they owe their time and dedication to the team, the school, their parents, and the community. They also have to know that you are willing to make the same commitment."

—Tim Brabant, Carsonville-Port Sanilac High School (MI)

"Your players need to trust you and buy in to the offensive and defensive schemes that you implement."

—Travis Cote, Bishop Guertin High School (NH)

"The one important aspect this year was trust. We had nine seniors that came together around week 5 and got better and better as the season went. By the playoffs, our kids trusted each other and had a ton of confidence. Take one game at a time, and don't let the outside sources impede with what the team wants to accomplish. Stay focused, and most importantly have fun."

—Larry Glatczak, Centralia/Wetmore High School (KS)

This stage is where it all comes together. The leadership, the mental toughness, coaching the heart of the athlete, developing the work ethic, creating team chemistry—none of these matters if the team does not trust you, their head coach. If the captain of the ship lacks the trust and confidence of his crew, it will lead to ineffectiveness and an inability to navigate his ship through the waters to the land of champions. When the head coach loses the trust and confidence of his players, coaches, administration, and community, he becomes nothing more than an obstacle for his team to reach peak performance.

The players must have trust and confidence in not only the head coach, but also his coaching staff, the X's and O's between the field, and the overall philosophy of the program. Do your players trust you? Do they have confidence in your systems? Do the other coaches on your staff trust you? Do the parents of your players have confidence that you are going to treat their sons the right way and develop them as young men? How about your administration? Do they have your back? Building trust and confidence takes time. It does not just happen overnight.

"Buy-in was our biggest difference. Our players bought into our system and believed in what we were doing in all aspects of our program. We didn't play anyone who was not willing to do what we asked and play where we asked them to. We didn't give up on them, but playing time was the reward that seemed to motivate best. Believing in something bigger than you was a theme that was also effective. Our team slogan is: 'Team, Pride, Trust,' and we were able to use that to keep us focused on our own goals."

—Kim Nelson, Roosevelt High School (SD)

"Trust. The most important characteristic of a great leader is that he can be trusted. Trust is developed by being honest, remaining consistent, and always following through with what you say you are going to do."

—Mike Favero, Logan (UT) High School

"Start with trust. Coaches trust each other, coaches trust players, and most importantly players must trust themselves, their teammates, and their coaches".

—Billy Kirch, Waverly-South Shore High School (SD)

Trust Is a Two-Way Street

"Do not be afraid to give the kids some ownership in what you do, and allow them to make plays by not limiting what they are truly capable of. We let the kids come up with the verbal calls to communicate the plays to the entire offense, and rarely did we have a missed assignment. When the kids had a suggestion, we listened. They took ownership, and we averaged about 45 points a game."

—Ray Steele, Indian River High School (DE)

"Pay attention to your players, and focus on trying to get the most out of them. You must put the toughest players on the field and play to their strengths. Flexibility in schemes is very important; don't try to force plays or schemes on them that they can't get. Motivate them daily with goals and themes for the week. If you believe in them, they will believe in you."

—Dan Higgins, Piscataway (NJ) High School

For the most part, teenagers today do not just automatically trust you because you are their head coach. They just do not have that automatic respect for the position anymore. You have to earn that trust as a person. Most of you reading this would have *never* questioned your head coach. Kids today are different. They want to be trusted just as much as you do. Trust is a two-way street. It is like a bank account. The more you put in to trusting the kids, the more you will be able to withdraw their trust in you. The more you give them ownership of the program, the more they will have trust and confidence in you as the leader.

They want to be trusted; they want to stand up and be responsible for their program. Find ways to do this in your program. I shared earlier in this book about the player committee that I have used for a long time. The committee is a great format to show the players I trust them. It is a way to help develop that two-way street of trust with the team.

Tell Them the Truth

"Confidence was the most important aspect of our league championship season. We fixed so many issues we had with our own fundamentals that one win after another, our confidence grew and we really began to believe in what we were doing. We got it right at the right time. We learned about ourselves early in the season and fixed 'us.' This is developed through hard work and continued positive reinforcement of good play performances."

—Bruce Kozerski, Holy Cross High School (KY)

Coach Kozerski brings up a great point about growing confidence in your players. Confidence grows as your players see themselves becoming better as the season progresses. The main way this happens is through film study and review. Are you honest with your players during film? Are you honest with your players about your upcoming opponent? Do not sugarcoat what you are facing in the next opponent. Doing so will make your players question you. If you fail to tell your players how good or bad the upcoming team is (if you are not watching film of them) and the kids go out and are surprised by what happens on Friday night, how do you think they will approach your comments the next time you give them a scouting report?

I have always believed in being very honest with my players. They will come to trust your judgment and your ability if you are up front with them. If you try to look past their mistakes in the film room, other players will know it; they will see right through it. You will lose credibility with the players. Don't be afraid to correct your kids. Doing so will not only make your team better, but they will gain confidence as they fix their technique week by week.

Give Your Kids Confidence in Practice

"Believe you can win (or have chance to win) every game. Extreme preparation and situations in practice."

—Mark Buderus, Florence (CO) High School

Nothing will give your players confidence on the field better than putting them in positions during the practice week that they will see on Friday night. For most of you, this is an absolute no-brainer. But I am always surprised to hear about programs that never practice game-specific situations their kids will be in. Do you format your practices in such a way that you move all over the field, and practice many different situations your kids might be in on Friday night?

I watched the 2008 California state champions, St. Margaret's Episcopal of San Juan Capistrano, practice during the championship week. Harry Welch was the head coach at the time. He has won three state championships with three different programs in California (Canyon, 2006; St. Margaret's, 2008 and Santa Margarita, 2011). They practiced field goals for about 30 minutes that day. I was surprised to see a team practice field goals for so long in their 15th week of the season. They practiced getting it blocked, they practiced bad snaps, they practiced fakes, everything. Coach Welch wanted his kids to be in perfect position should they go through any of these scenarios on game night.

Building confidence in your players during practice is a key to getting the most out of them on Friday night. I have seen so many coaches try to just throw something in on Thursday and expect kids to execute it flawlessly on Friday night. It just does not work that way. They need the confidence of repetitions. I have a play in my playbook for two-point conversions that my kids gave the name "Money" a few years ago because it worked so well in practice. They had so much confidence in this play that the first time we were in the position where we needed two points, what do you think they yelled at me on the sidelines?

Putting together a practice script is the key to making sure that your coaching staff puts your kids in many different positions on the practice field to build their confidence. Many coaches can get in the rut of just running their offensive team time for 40 minutes between the 30-yard lines. They never put their team in down-and-distance situations. Practice red zone offense, red zone defense, third-and-long, fourth-and-short, your fake punts, kicking after a safety, etc. If you do not write this down in a practice script, you probably will not practice it.

Do What You Say, and Say What You Do

Trust is like respect: you don't just get it; you must earn it. Gaining the trust of your players will happen if you are a consistent person. As the head coach, you must do what you say and say what you do. Your players and coaching staff will learn to trust that your word is your bond over a period of time of you doing what you say you will do. You have probably all worked for someone in your life who failed to do this. You learned that you could not trust their word. They never followed through on meeting plans, and simply blew off doing things they committed to. Those people are not fun to follow. Once you lose trust in a person, you stop respecting them. Building trust in your players starts with doing what you say you will do.

A major part of this idea of doing what you say and saying what you do comes in the form of following through on team policies and procedures. Nothing will destroy the trust and confidence of your team more than treating players differently. If you tell your players that they will run two laps if they are late, make every athlete who is late run two laps. If you have a rule about what to wear to practice, and your starting quarterback fails to wear the right pants to practice, you have a choice. Discipline him as per your team policy, or let it slide because you don't want to alienate the star. If you fail to discipline kids because they are stars, your non-stars are going to learn not to trust your word. If you tell the team during film on Saturday, "Anyone late on Monday runs," and then fail to follow through, kids will see this, and they will not trust or respect you.

Among Your Coaching Staff

If you are a head coach who is reading this book, let me ask you this question: how is the trust and confidence amongst your staff? Do they trust you? Do they have confidence in you? Have you ever asked them about this? Creating trust and confidence amongst your staff is just as important—some might argue it is more important—as developing it amongst your troops. It's vital that every coach on your staff trusts not only you, but each other. It's crucial that you have confidence in one another. I've made a few questionable hires in my time as a head coach. Sometimes, you never know until you get into the meat of your schedule how a coach will turn out. It is an awful feeling, working with someone day in and day out that you do not have trust and confidence in.

Back in 2003, my good friend and a mentor of mine, Perry Krosschell, resigned his position as head football coach at Linfield Christian. I was on the staff with about eight other guys. I was the newest member there. However, I was the head junior varsity coach, and Coach Krosschell was told me that he wanted me to have the job. He told me that he had recommended me to the administration to take over. I was not sure what the others on the staff thought about this. Most of the staff were walk-on coaches, and just weren't around much during the off-season. I was coaching varsity baseball at the time, and I will never forget one day when the defensive coordinator, Bear Schoolmeester, stopped by baseball practice to talk about the football coach search. I did not really know at the time where he was with the idea of me taking over.

Bear is a great football coach, one of the best I've ever been around. So, his opinion mattered more to me than any of the other coaches in the program. He was the most seasoned out of all of them. I had only known him for about a year and a half at this point, not real well yet. I was nervous as he came up and said, "Coach, need to chat with you about the head football job." I thought maybe he wanted it; he had coached for far longer than I had at this point. But he said to me, "They better pick you for this job. Perry told me he recommended you. Dude, you are the perfect fit for this job." All of a sudden, with Coach Bear's approval, I had all of the confidence in the world. He trusted me; he had confidence in me to become his boss. That meant the world to me. We are great friends to this day. He has been my defensive coordinator longer than anyone else. In fact, when I left that school in 2006, he came to help me out at another school when the defensive coordinator there was struggling. He drove three hours round trip to come help our football team that year. Now that is a dedicated man. It all started with having trust and confidence in each other as assistant coaches working side by side, and it built over the years. You have got to have that kind of trust and confidence in each other. As the head coach, it is your job to make it happen.

More Thoughts on Trust and Confidence

"Team unity and faith as one unit. Our team believed that it was possible to win. Belief doesn't always do it alone; however, it's a good start. I'm not talking about being cocky or overconfident; I'm merely talking about working hard and believing in each other's ability within that team. We preached team unity and practiced team unity. I believe team unity is a big part of team success."

—Ken Lucas, Annapolis Area Christian School (MD)

"I think the biggest difference for us was the attitude of the program. Not just from the players, but everyone in the program. The program established the goal of winning our second championship in a row, and it was the focus of all that we did. We all believed. Every lift in the weight, every lap and every rep in practice, every fundraiser, and every meal for the team was about being a champion. Everyone also believed that we were going to be champions; therefore, practice, games, booster meetings, and everything else had a meaning. We were, I believe, the best conditioned team, allowing us persevere when our opponents wilted late in the game. Our players were the most determined team."

—Jim Hartman, Yarmouth (ME) High School

"Belief in each other, the system, and the goal. Absolutely the difference. I think that in order to develop that belief, we just walked it, preached it, and lived it. With positive attitudes from everyone involved. We do not allow a negative thought to be spoken or acted upon. Using the word 'can't' is immediate laps."

—Jim Hartman, Yarmouth (ME) High School

"Our kids believe they are going to make it to the finals and win every season. We talk from day one about making it to the finals, and anything else would be a disappointment. We have a great tradition, which helps us a great deal because every group doesn't want to be the team to disappoint past players who built this program. We talk about that daily."

—Mark Gibson, Bismarck (ND) High School

"Our football team expects to win every time they step on the field. This has been developed by years of hard work and dedication to our program. We believe we outprepare every opponent we face. We do this by our off-season and summer programs and also intense film study of our opponents through the week. One of our favorite quotes

is 'The will to prepare to win must be greater than the will to win.' In this year's playoffs alone, we won two games by two and two games by three. We were losing in the fourth quarter in three of the four games. We just believe we will always find a way."

—Jeff Craddock, Tarboro (NC) High School

"I think the most important part was attitude. South Pointe has been successful in football since the school opened only seven short years ago. Our players know that we have gained that success because of their basic God-given athletic ability. This year, I challenged our players by asking them, 'How good could you be?' The players knew they had to change their attitude to reach their best potential. That change in attitude created a better work ethic, more team unity, more dedication, and more individual character, which I believe is imperative to winning."

—Strait Herron, South Pointe High School (SC)

"Confidence and believing we could win. Something that has been produced through the years that the seniors continue to carry to the next team."

—Chris Miller, Byrnes High School (SC)

Time-Out

1. How do you currently build trust and confidence in your program? Do you have any systems in place to do this?
2. Did you have any issues with trust and confidence this last season? If so, why do you think those problems persisted?
3. Travis Cote, head coach at Bishop Guertin in New Hampshire said, "Your players need to trust you and buy into the offensive and defensive schemes that you implement." If I stepped foot on your campus tomorrow, would your players tell me that they have bought in to your systems? Why or why not?
4. Think of a time that you failed to make your word your bond. What were the results of that with your players? Having just read this chapter on building trust and confidence, how would you have handled that situation differently?
5. Do you have written team rules, policies, and procedures? Do you stick to those for the sake of everyone in your program?

Appendix

Survey Responses From Contributing State Champion Head Football Coaches

Note: All the coaches surveyed were sent the same three questions. Some responded to each question separately, while others provided one general reply. Their responses are included in this appendix in the format in which they were received, and all three questions are repeated in each coach's profile for ease of reference.

Alabama AISA Division AAA

Coach: Josh Wright

School: Bessemer Academy

City: Bessemer

2011 Record: 12-1, 5-1

Championship Game Results:

Bessemer	35
Glenwood (Phenix City)	21

State Championships at School: 5

Years as Head Coach: 5

Years at Current School: 5

State Championships Won as Head Coach: 1

What did you do differently this year from the other programs in your league, your section, your state that enabled your success as a state champion?

I think one of the best things we did this year was have our summer conditioning during the hottest times of the day. We would start workouts at 1:00 p.m. and go until 4:00, four days a week. We never had a heat problem or a cramp. We have water on the field at every station. The kids were used to the heat, and it helped a lot. Plus, the kids have already eaten; most of them twice. When we did early morning workouts, it was always a food issue or parents being late in traffic. At this time of the day, the kid doesn't have many excuses for being late.

What piece of advice would you give to a head coach who wants to win a state championship?

I would say make sure you surround yourself with the best people you can, and coach them up on how you want things done. Always accept responsibility, and do not lay blame on coaches or players. Keep all distractions away from your program and players. Make sure you do the right thing always, no matter what the cost.

What do you consider the one most important aspect of your championship team this year? How did you develop that in your program?

Discipline that makes sense to your players. Sometimes, as coaches, we ask kids to do things that don't make sense to them, and they rebel because of it. A lot of today's kids do not have the discipline they need at home, so we tried to instill it here. The team concept was our most important aspect. For instance, if a kid got in trouble during school, the entire team was punished after practice. After one incident, our football players were policing each other all over school in the classroom, and it spilled over to the field. We stopped having penalties, and our team became closer. A lot of selfishness started to disappear, and a different attitude transformed on the whole team.

Alabama Division 2A

Coach: Scott Rials

School: Elba High School

City: Elba

2011 Record: 15-0, 7-0

Championship Game Results:

Elba	34
Tanner	14

State Championships at School: 3

Years as Head Coach: 14

Years at Current School: 8

State Championships Won as Head Coach: 1

What did you do differently this year from the other programs in your league, your section, your state that enabled your success as a state champion?

We run the spread no-huddle offense. This seems to be a big plus for us because it allows us to put pressure on the defense. We use our same personnel with different formations. The no-huddle gives us an advantage in that we can dictate tempo.

What piece of advice would you give to a head coach who wants to win a state championship?

Be well prepared, and have a sound plan. You must have more than one plan in case things don't go as well as you hope for. Keep your plan simple so adjustments can be made at any time.

What do you consider the one most important aspect of your championship team this year? How did you develop that in your program?

Togetherness. Our players have been playing on the same team for several years. Each player has the other ones back at all times. This was developed through a sound strength and conditioning program and Fellowship of Christian Athletes. Trust is of the utmost importance.

Alabama Division 5A

Coach: Bob Godsey

School: Hartselle High School

City: Hartselle

2011 Record: 15-0, 7-0

Championship Game Results:

| Hartselle | 13 |
| Vigor (Prichard) | 3 |

State Championships at School: 1

Years as Head Coach: 14

Years at Current School: 9

State Championships Won as Head Coach: 1

What did you do differently this year from the other programs in your league, your section, your state that enabled your success as a state champion?

I think we spend more time on ourselves. We are not a big athletic or imposing team. Our edge has to be execution. We must outexecute our opponent. Our kids really bought into that this year in all phases of the game. When we needed it most, we seemed to execute at our very best.

What piece of advice would you give to a head coach who wants to win a state championship?

One piece of advice is to understand that, to win it all in Alabama, it is a 15-game schedule. For years, we prepared for a 10-game, and were worn out by the end of the regular season. You must pace yourself, your staff, and most importantly your team for this 15-week grind. We often overwork our teams from fear of not being ready. I am talking more from a mental standpoint than a physical. Find times in the season to take days off or go lighter than normal in hopes that it will keep them fresh for a long playoff run.

What do you consider the one most important aspect of your championship team this year? How did you develop that in your program?

Team chemistry. We have good team chemistry year in and year out in our program, but this team bonded like no other. When you assemble nearly 100 teenage boys from all walks of life, things are going to happen. Not all players are going to see everything the same way. But this team, during practice and games, was able to put their differences aside for the good of all. Not all people (teams) are willing to do that. Teammates helped each other make good decisions. When poor decisions were made, teammates handled it and worked hard to prevent it from happening again. The poor decision-makers appreciated the effort of their teammates and made great efforts to improve their own decisions. In turn, the effort to improve was noticed by all, which resulted in a unified team. This was most evident by the play of our team in crucial late-game situations. In the end, they were able to put differences or issues aside for the good of the team.

Alaska Large School Division

Coach: Jason Caldarera
School: Service High School
City: Anchorage
2011 Record: 10-0-1, 7-0

Championship Game Results:

    Service   37
    South (Anchorage)   23

State Championships at School: 6

Years as Head Coach: 12

Years at Current School: 19

State Championships Won as Head Coach: 2

Noteworthy: After the 2011 season, Service High School was ranked #1 in the state. In addition, the school had won more state championships than any other school in Alaska.

What did you do differently this year from the other programs in your league, your section, your state that enabled your success as a state champion?

It is difficult to get student-athletes exposure in Alaska. We had a dynamic group of players this year that we wanted to expose to a higher level of football and expand their perspective of competitive football across the country. After a year's worth of planning and fundraising, we traveled to play Leilehua High school on Oahu, Hawaii. They are a perennial powerhouse in Hawaii, and we earned a lot of respect playing them to a 34-34 tie in what was broadcasted as the "Fire and Ice Bowl." Service High School came back from that first game to play with a sense of urgency and a fast tempo game plan that resonated in our undefeated season 10-0-1, culminating in a 2011 Cook Inlet Conference Championship and Alaska State Large Schools Football Championship.

What piece of advice would you give to a head coach who wants to win a state championship?

Have a vision of where you want the program to be—immediately, a year from now, and a few years from now. Surround yourself with competent, quality people on the football staff and in the parent group to help get you there. It is impossible to do everything well by yourself. Implement structured year-round training opportunities, but encourage your kids to compete in everything they can. Foster the team-family concept from your lower levels on up, so that they will give the effort and hard work it takes to be a part of successful program.

What do you consider the one most important aspect of your championship team this year? How did you develop that in your program?

Our philosophy at Service has always been to develop young student-athletes that make good decisions on and off the field. People that buy in to the Cougar Family concept know that on top of their athleticism, it is quality of character that overcomes trials and tribulations, that determines a champion. We preach that in order to overcome adversity, we have to do it together as a team, not as individuals. We battle unique elements in Alaska—the distance, the cost, the short season due to inclement weather. It helps to have year-round contact with kids, following academic progress, instituting a structured speed strength program, and skills clinics. More importantly, we have created a great football culture with high expectations for all involved, including coaches, players, and parents.

Arizona Division IV

Coach: Paul Moro

School: Blue Ridge High School

City: Lakeside

2011 Record: 14-0, 7-0

Championship Game Results:

| Blue Ridge | 35 |
| Show Low | 14 |

State Championships at School: 15

Years as Head Coach: 29

Years at Current School: 29

State Championships Won as Head Coach: 12

What did you do differently this year from the other programs in your league, your section, your state that enabled your success as a state champion?

I do not pay attention to what the other schools are doing. We just try to get our players to play hard and smart.

What piece of advice would you give to a head coach who wants to win a state championship?

Find a mentor who can help you overcome all the obstacles that you face yearly.

What do you consider the one most important aspect of your championship team this year? How did you develop that in your program?

Team unity. We try to develop a servanthood type of philosophy. Jesus has given us all a great example of this. Those that are last shall be first. This means that those who serve others will reap the rewards of life.

Arizona Division 1

Coach: Dan Hinds

School: Desert Vista High School

City: Phoenix

2011 Record: 13-1, 3-0

Championship Game Results:

| Desert Vista | 45 |
| Hamilton (Chandler) | 19 |

State Championships at School: 2

Years as Head Coach: 10

Years at Current School: 10

State Championships Won as Head Coach: 1

Noteworthy: After the 2011 season, Desert Vista High School was ranked #1 in the state.

What did you do differently this year from the other programs in your league, your section, your state that enabled your success as a state champion?

What we do differently than most other big schools in Arizona is our offensive schemes. We run the fly offense, quarterback under the center about 70 percent of the time. Some of the advantages to this offense are:

- It seems to give your line better angles. With a smaller offensive line, this as an advantage. We beat Hamilton, who clearly had us outmatched, but with the angles and deception created by the fly, we were able to move the ball.
- By putting your most athletic player at the fly position, it forces defenses to make adjustments to the fly. If they do not adjust and keep seven men in the box, keep running the fly. When they do make an adjustment, other things come open (inside run, counter, play-action, etc.).
- Opposing coaches have said that trying to simulate the fly in practice with their scout team is difficult. Not very many teams in Arizona run it; therefore, their players have no exposure to it, and do not really understand how it works.

What piece of advice would you give to a head coach who wants to win a state championship?

I am not one to give unsolicited advice, so I guess I would say, "Be true to yourself," meaning don't let others try to get you to do things with your program that you don't feel comfortable doing. It's your program; run it how you think it should be run, not how others might think you should run it.

What do you consider the one most important aspect of your championship team this year? How did you develop that in your program?

The most significant aspect of this team I believe was a tremendously strong group of senior leaders who trusted each other, and trusted us as coaches. How we developed this, well, I believe that we got dealt a good hand, and it all came together for us. We coaches presented the team with ways to get better prepared, starting in our off-season workouts, and they bought it, and continued to buy in all the way to the final week of preparation. Our game plan was complex, and different than anything we had done all year, but they bought it. This was the most prepared team I have ever coached.

California Division 2

Coach: Troy Starr

School: Helix High School

City: La Mesa

2011 Record: 13-1, 5-0

Championship Game Results:

    Helix   35

    Del Oro (Loomis)   24

State Championships at School: 1*

Years as Head Coach: 18

Years at Current School: 4

State Championships Won as Head Coach: 1

What did you do differently this year from the other programs in your league, your section, your state that enabled your success as a state champion?

We use Urban Meyer's comprehensive plan for football, it's the fourth year we've used it. It's called "Plan to Win." Marshall, Temple, Louisville—they are all using it. It's a great overall plan. Plan to Win is the foundation for what we do. It shrinks the gap between the most invested and the least invested kid in your program. You get invested kids; a kid who isn't invested can't be a part of your program. They are all extremely bought in.

What piece of advice would you give to a head coach who wants to win a state championship?

I just came back from the University of Florida, where I spent a year working with Urban Meyer; I was the director of football operations. My office was right next to his. I got to

*Note: California started a state championship format in 2006.

watch this Plan to Win program in action every day. The program works. It's broken down in to four quarters, and the plan works. Play great defense, score in the red zone, win the special teams battle, protect the football; if you do those four, you are going to win. Four easy things, but when you have to have all of the drills, and the details to do that, you have to focus on these things. It can't be just lip service. Try to load the defense as much as possible with the best players. Where I made mistakes earlier with some of my teams is: I thought you could win with offense; it doesn't work like that.

What do you consider the one most important aspect of your championship team this year? How did you develop that in your program?

The most important aspect was that we spent an incredible amount of time, whole practice sessions, scoring in the red zone and goal line. We worked on red zone offense, and defense in the red zone. We probably spent more time than any team in the state in the red zone. Those huge games at the end of the year, the difference in the red zone is huge. We had a very complete plan for the red zone. We would practice with a star out with an injury. We practiced and prepared for any of those crazy, real-life scenarios. 30 seconds, one time-out, ball at the 9—all of those different scenarios.

California Division 1

Coach: Harry Welch

School: Santa Margarita Catholic High School

City: Rancho Santa Margarita

2011 Record: 13-2, 3-2

Championship Game Results:

Santa Margarita	42
Bellarmine (San Jose)	37

State Championships at School: 1*

Years as Head Coach: 24

Years at Current School: 2

State Championships Won as Head Coach: 3

Noteworthy: After the 2011 season, Santa Margarita Catholic High School was ranked #2 in the state. The 2011 state championship was Coach Welch's third, with three different schools: Canyon, St. Margaret's, and Santa Margarita.

*Note: California started a state championship format in 2006.

What did you do differently this year from the other programs in your league, your section, your state that enabled your success as a state champion?

I am not aware of what other schools do; I focus on my own program.

What piece of advice would you give to a head coach who wants to win a state championship?

Be yourself. Do not focus on winning a state championship. Focus on daily excellence.

What do you consider the one most important aspect of your championship team this year? How did you develop that in your program?

Accountability is the most important aspect of our championship season. Work on it with players, coaches, and yourself every day.

California Division 4

Coach: Jon Ellinghouse

School: Sierra Canyon High School

City: Chatsworth

2011 Record: 15-0, 6-0

Championship Game Results:

| Sierra Canyon | 34 |
| Le Grand | 13 |

State Championships at School: 1

Years as Head Coach: 4

Years at Current School: 4

State Championships Won as Head Coach: 1

What did you do differently this year from the other programs in your league, your section, your state that enabled your success as a state champion?

I would say, more so than any other time in my career, I let go of many of the aspects of my program. As a young coach, the hardest thing to do is learn to delegate and trust other coaches. I didn't have to do it all myself, and that made every aspect of my program better. It made me a better head coach. I hired some of the best coaches around, and let them be themselves (inside of my vision). Sierra Canyon is a small school, and we try to allow our players to have fun, and allow their personalities to come out through their play. Another key reason that I believe we won is that our program and school is only four years old; four years ago, I played many freshmen on the varsity level. It was a tough year, but we made it a success. That paid off so big because the kids on the field for us this year were experienced veterans who had seen it all. It is very rare that you have a junior playing that has 41 games experience. We had that all over the field, and I believe that set us apart.

What piece of advice would you give to a head coach who wants to win a state championship?

I believe the biggest task of a head coach in high school athletics is creating a mindset and an expectation in your players. You have to get them to believe that they are doing it better and working harder than anyone else. If you get a kid coached up well, there is a high likelihood he will be successful, but if you get a passionate kid coached up well, he is unstoppable. A state championship season is a very long haul. The kids have to want to be back at practice on Monday for the 16th week of the season; if they don't, it will come out in their play.

What do you consider the one most important aspect of your championship team this year? How did you develop that in your program?

I feel we did the little things right. You can't just coach the big picture, because the big picture is made from several little pictures. We had a tight-knit group of kids that bought into a common goal. We also had the most talented team I have ever coached.

Colorado Division 5A

Coach: Andy Lowry

School: Columbine High School

City: Littleton

2011 Record: 14-0, 5-0

Championship Game Results:

| Columbine | 41 |
| Lakewood | 31 |

State Championships at School: 5

Years as Head Coach: 20

Years at Current School: 18

State Championships Won as Head Coach: 5

Noteworthy: After the 2011 season, Columbine High School was ranked #2 in the state.

What did you do differently this year from the other programs in your league, your section, your state that enabled your success as a state champion?

I don't know what we did differently from other programs, but I give a ton of credit to my assistant coaches. They do a great job of teaching and building relationships with our kids. Winning a championship takes some luck with injuries, turnovers, official's calls, and lucky or unlucky breaks. This year, our team was healthy at the right time, and we were fortunate with the bounces and breaks. Our team had two great running backs, and our entire team improved every week throughout the playoffs.

What piece of advice would you give to a head coach who wants to win a state championship?

My advice would be to coach one week at a time, and don't make it about a championship. When teams work to improve each and every day, championships take care of themselves. Championships are a result of bringing a group of kids together, motivating them, and getting them to believe in each other and what your coaches are selling. Coach's jobs are to teach, motivate, and try to get a group of kids to become the best team that they can be. Our coaches are great teachers and are men of faith. I believe their faith keeps them humble, and the concept of serving others serves as great role models for the kids. Their walk of faith keeps life in perspective and encourages our athletes to use the lessons learned in football in their everyday life. God has blessed us with good kids and with great opportunities in this profession.

What do you consider the one most important aspect of your championship team this year? How did you develop that in your program?

I think something we did very well this year was to get our kids to buy into concentrating on details and little things. Little things make big differences. Focusing on the little things helps with execution, penalties, and preparing kids in making plays. Hopefully, these all lead to real life. Selling the kids on hard work, commitment, and selflessness builds teams and young men. Relating character to life as a husband, father, employee, and person of faith helps young people understand the commitment they are making in sports is helping them grow as a person. If the kids can concentrate on little things, they have the ability to focus on the details of every play and every assignment. This started from day 1 during stretches, warm-ups, and everyday drills. We continued to demand the little things throughout the entire playoffs and during warm-ups in the state championship game.

Colorado 2A

Coach: Mark Buderus
School: Florence High School

City: Florence

2011 Record: 13-1, 5-1

Championship Game Results:

    Florence   34

    Bayfield   0

State Championships at School: 5

Years as Head Coach: 31

Years at Current School: 27

State Championships Won as Head Coach: 3

What did you do differently this year from the other programs in your league, your section, your state that enabled your success as a state champion?

Stayed healthy/stayed the course/played the best ball the last four weeks.

What piece of advice would you give to a head coach who wants to win a state championship?

Stay the course/don't change just to change/consistency and routine in the things you do.

What do you consider the one most important aspect of your championship team this year? How did you develop that in your program?

Believe you can win (or have chance to win) every game/extreme preparation and situations in practice.

Delaware Division 2

Coach: Ray Steele

School: Indian River High School

City: Dagsboro

2011 Record: 12-0, 6-0

Championship Game Results:

    Indian Rive   35

    Caravel (Bear)   13

State Championships at School: 2

Years as Head Coach: 1

Years at Current School: 1

State Championships Won as Head Coach: 1

Noteworthy: After the 2011 season, Indian River High School was ranked #3 in the state. Before becoming head coach, Steele was an assistant coach at Indian River High School for 35 years.

What did you do differently this year from the other programs in your league, your section, your state that enabled your success as a state champion?

This year, we ran a speed-up no-huddle offense and let our quarterback call 95 percent of the plays from scrimmage. This gave us a tremendous advantage on the field. We ran that offense in practice and could get in 60 to 80 plays in a 25-minute offensive segment. It not only made practice upbeat and fun, but it was great conditioning.

What piece of advice would you give to a head coach who wants to win a state championship?

Do not be afraid to give the kids some ownership in what you do, and allow them to make plays by not limiting what they are truly capable of. We let the kids come up with the verbal calls to communicate the plays to the entire offense, and rarely did we have a missed assignment. When the kids had a suggestion, we listened. They took ownership, and we averaged about 45 points a game.

What do you consider the one most important aspect of your championship team this year? How did you develop that in your program?

The most important aspect would have to be the leadership from our seniors. Everyone bought into the conditioning and team concept because everyone saw our seniors working as hard as they could to just win. No one came into the season with a preset agenda—just to win and have fun playing.

Delaware Division 1

Coach: Mark DelPercio

School: Middletown High School

City: Middletown

2011 Record: 11-2, 7-2

Championship Game Results:

| Middletown | 27 |
| Newark | 23 |

State Championships at School: 6

Years as Head Coach: 14

Years at Current School: 18

State Championships Won as Head Coach: 2

What did you do differently this year from the other programs in your league, your section, your state that enabled your success as a state champion?

We provided the structure and program for our players to work their tail off. Hard work equals success.

What piece of advice would you give to a head coach who wants to win a state championship?

Focus on what you need to do to win football games. Too often, coaches focus on the wrong things, and the extra fluff will not help you win games.

What do you consider the one most important aspect of your championship team this year? How did you develop that in your program?

Chemistry that was developed during the off-season and season with our team-building activities. We do not spend time on the things that do not impact our play on the field, such as the way we look (no fancy uniforms) or fancy website. This only allows for opponents to do some easy research on us.

Team activities. I take them bowling once/year when we hit a wall with practice. This could be pre-season or in-season. We also do a "if you really knew me" activity during the pre-season so we can get to know each other better.

Florida Division 1A

Coach: Jeremy Brown

School: Jefferson County High School

City: Monticello

2011 Record: 10-5, 4-0

Championship Game Results:

Jefferson County	47
Chipley	13

State Championships at School: 6

Years as Head Coach: 2

Years at Current School: 2

State Championships Won as Head Coach: 1

Noteworthy: The 2011 Championship was Jefferson County High School's first in 20 years.

What did you do differently this year from the other programs in your league, your section, your state that enabled your success as a state champion?

I truly believe the one thing that sets our program apart from other programs is our commitment to coaching the heart of the athlete. Most coaches get so caught up in the X's and O's, but they never spend time coaching the heart of their kids. Our program is very involved in the Fellowship of Christian Athletes, and we focus on giving our football team a Christ-centered foundation that will last long after football is over. We pray together, read bible scripture together, and attend church together once a month as a team. We also spend time together just hanging out as team while having Madden tournaments, playing cards, watching movies, and going bowling as a team. I truly believe the time we as coaches invest in our players off the football field is what drives them to give us so much effort on Friday nights. In today's society, we are seeing more and more kids coming from single-parent homes, where most are single-mother households, so as a coach we have to fill this void as a father figure for our kids. I have players in my home on a consistent basis so they can see what a successful and functional family looks like. Ultimately, what we as coaches should be teaching our kids is so much bigger than just football.

What piece of advice would you give to a head coach who wants to win a state championship?

Obviously, you have to a great off-season program and fundamentally sound offensive, defensive, and special team philosophies. But most teams have that. I believe it is the execution of these philosophies and the effort players give that makes any scheme or philosophy work. I feel the best way to assure that your team plays with an extreme sense of focus and effort is to spend more time coaching their hearts and less time coaching their bodies. Ultimately, your players have to know you love and care about them more than just a football player.

What do you consider the one most important aspect of your championship team this year? How did you develop that in your program?

I believe we had a great group of young men that bought into the product we as coaches sold them. We constantly talked about being uncommon—both on and off the field. In most schools today, being late to class, being lazy in class, and being disrespectful to teachers is more prevalent than it's ever been, so we talk to our kids about being uncommon or abnormal on campus, getting to class on time, giving great effort, and being respectful to your teachers. This attitude of being uncommon really carried over to the football program; we had more kids with 100 percent attendance in our summer weight program, we didn't have players missing practice, and ultimately our kids played with an extreme amount of emotion and effort at practice and on game night. We tested our team's toughness and commitment to the program by playing seven teams who were in larger classifications, three of which ended up playing for the 2A, 3A, and 5A state championships. By doing this, we started the season 1-4, and I believe most teams would have folded, players would have started blaming each other for the losses, and some probably would have quit. But the foundation we had built combined with the relationships we as coaches had with our guys allowed our team to stay close as team, and although we had those tough losses, we continued to get better each week. Our faith in Christ, the trust we had for each other, and the effort our kids played with is what allowed us to capture the Florida 1A Football state championship.

Florida 7A

Coach: Joe Kinnan

School: Manatee High School

City: Bradenton

2011 Record: 13-2, 3-0

Championship Game Results:

| Manatee | 40 |
| First Coast (Jacksonville) | 0 |

State Championships at School: 5

Years as Head Coach: 30

Years at Current School: 27

State Championships Won as Head Coach: 5

Noteworthy: After the 2011 season, Manatee High School was ranked #1 in the state and #8 in the nation.

What did you do differently this year from the other programs in your league, your section, your state that enabled your success as a state champion?

One thing we did differently this year from other teams in our league and state was our leadership council and character development program.

What piece of advice would you give to a head coach who wants to win a state championship?

Sell players on your system, and teach them something other than football.

What do you consider the one most important aspect of your championship team this year? How did you develop that in your program?

Revised strength and conditioning program.

Florida Division 2A

Coach: Robert Craft

School: North Florida Christian School

City: Tallahassee

2011 Record: 13-0, 1-0

Championship Game Results:

| North Florida Christian School | 69 |
| Admiral Farragut (St. Petersburg) | 0 |

State Championships at School: 7

Years as Head Coach: 2

Years at Current School: 2

State Championships Won as Head Coach: 1

What did you do differently this year from the other programs in your league, your section, your state that enabled your success as a state champion?

I believe our off-season strength and conditioning program is outstanding. Our coaches spend a lot of time researching what is best for our team and athletes. Our coaches spend time organizing these workouts so our kids get the most out of every workout. Our in-season practice schedule and organization is typically better than most in our league. We film all practices, and both our coaches and players watch those practices. This time of review and instruction is very important.

What piece of advice would you give to a head coach who wants to win a state championship?

Outwork your opponents. Be productive and efficient in all that you do. Find ways that will separate you and your team from your opponents. Find ways to consistently challenge your team to compete. Leave no stone unturned.

What do you consider the one most important aspect of your championship team this year? How did you develop that in your program?

Our senior leadership was the biggest difference in our team in 2011 compared to other teams we have had. Our seniors' leadership and work ethic was outstanding; it made them better every day and made everyone around them better, too. Every year, I spend a lot of time in the off-season with our seniors trying to develop them as leaders, believing that our success in the fall will be based on their leadership.

Florida Division 8A

Coach: Robert Weiner

School: Plant High School

City: Tampa

2011 Record: 14-1, 3-0

Championship Game Results:

Plant	31
Miramar	20

State Championships at School: 4

Years as Head Coach: 8

Years at Current School: 8

State Championships Won as Head Coach: 4

Noteworthy: After the 2011 season, Plant High School was ranked #3 in the state and #9 in the nation.

What did you do differently this year from the other programs in your league, your section, your state that enabled your success as a state champion?

Plant High School is a very unique place with amazing academics, athletics, and community support. I know that it sounds cliché, but I believe our success in winning the state championship this year (and winning it four times in the last six years) was due to getting all of the various elements to be moving in the same direction at the same time. We had an incredible group of players who have dedicated themselves to excellence in the classroom (we have won the county football team academic award for six consecutive years), inspiration in the community, and—with the commitment of outstanding assistant coaches—ultimate achievement on the football field. This year, we had an extraordinary group of young whose leadership was beyond compare. We certainly did not have the most talented players this year, but we were without question the best team—a group that made everyone proud in so many ways.

What piece of advice would you give to a head coach who wants to win a state championship?

Again, I am not sure that I have any incredible wisdom or magic dust in this regard. We, as a program, do have a vision for our young people. We all—players, coaches, and supporters—take pride in believing that we work. All of our people have bought into the idea that nothing is ever given, and if it is, we don't want it anyway. So we are always going to try to work our hardest in every little aspect to make sure that our players are maximizing their potential as students, as people, and as players. In my opinion, the most important elements for the head coach is that I try to be caring, detail-oriented, and organized. The players and assistant coaches must know clearly what your team vision is, and only then can everyone apply their personal gifts to those goals.

What do you consider the one most important aspect of your championship team this year? How did you develop that in your program?

In my opinion, our team unity was the most important aspect and impacted everything we did. From dealing with early season tragedies within our football family to on-the-field battles, our team has always been together, a group of young people who care more about us and each other than they do about themselves. We have a program that we call the "link in chain." Each one of our players gets a karabiner link at the beginning of the season that is a tangible representation that he is a teammate. Each team member carries this link wherever he goes. All players always sign any correspondence to each other with the words "Always a link." This is a sign and symbol of our unity.

Florida Division 6A

Coach: Sean Callahan

School: Armwood High School

City: Seffner

2011 Record: 15-0, 6-0

Championship Game Results:

| Armwood | 40 |
| Central (Miami) | 31 |

State Championships at School: 3

Years as Head Coach: 21

Years at Current School: 28

State Championships Won as Head Coach: 3

Noteworthy: After the 2011 season, Armwood High School was ranked #3 in the nation.

What did you do differently this year from the other programs in your league, your section, your state that enabled your success as a state champion?

We did nothing differently. With the success we have had, it has caused us to work harder to continually challenge ourselves more (raise the bar).

What piece of advice would you give to a head coach who wants to win a state championship?

Create competition amongst your team, position by position. Try not to let anyone be comfortable with his position (status). A lot of hard work in what you believe. To have a staff that believes in you and the course that you have laid out, and a lot of patience. Be positive and consistent in your day-to-day approach, too.

What do you consider the one most important aspect of your championship team this year? How did you develop that in your program?

We were very mature, a lot of talented seniors (12 players signed D1A on the national signing day). We had to deal with adversity, and you have to handle it correctly, and we did.

Georgia Division AA

Coach: Hal Lamb

School: Calhoun High School

City: Calhoun

2011 Record: 15-0, 7-0

Championship Game Results:

    Calhoun   27 (in overtime)
    Buford   24

State Championships at School: 2

Years as Head Coach: 15

Years at Current School: 13

State Championships Won as Head Coach: 1

What did you do differently this year from the other programs in your league, your section, your state that enabled your success as a state champion?

I think our off-season program really got us over the top mentally and physically. Mentally, I think our kids believed they could beat anybody because of the work they put in during the off-season.

What piece of advice would you give to a head coach who wants to win a state championship?

Stay the course. Believe in what you do and how you do it.

What do you consider the one most important aspect of your championship team this year? How did you develop that in your program?

Definitely our team chemistry. Our kids really cared and loved each other.

Georgia Division AAAAA

Coach: Mickey Conn

School: Grayson

City: Loganville

2011 Record: 15-0, 8-0

Championship Game Results:

    Grayson   24
    Walton (Marrieta) 0

State Championships at School: 1

Years as Head Coach: 12

Years at Current School: 12

State Championships Won as Head Coach: 1

What did you do differently this year from the other programs in your league, your section, your state that enabled your success as a state champion?

I don't know what other programs do, so that is a difficult question to answer.

What piece of advice would you give to a head coach who wants to win a state championship?

I would first tell the coach to work on his relationship with God through Jesus Christ. It is important to communicate with God through prayer and scripture in order to have a clear picture of how God would want you to lead your team. The next thing is to build a team. A coach must do as much team-building activities as possible. It is important that your players become unselfish. This is a tough process due to all the media attention given to our sport, but one that is attainable. A coach must have a schematic philosophy and stick to it regardless of influences around him. Keep your game plan simple, and don't overcoach your players. Allow them to understand and play fast. If they are thinking too much, they will not play fast. Don't change your routines or do anything special during your playoff run. You have not won anything until you win the final championship game; then, have parades and pep rallies.

What do you consider the one most important aspect of your championship team this year? How did you develop that in your program?

This year's team was very unselfish. It did not matter who got the credit as long as our team got the victory. That is a special trait. I am not sure I did anything differently. This team just listened.

Georgia GISA Division AA

Coach: Rhett Farmer

School: Piedmont Academy

City: Monticello

2011 Record: 13-0, 6-0

Championship Game Results:

Piedmont Academy	13
Burke Academy	8

State Championships at School: 2

Years as Head Coach: 5

Years at Current School: 3

State Championships Won as Head Coach: 2

What did you do differently this year from the other programs in your league, your section, your state that enabled your success as a state champion?

One thing that we do differently compared to other teams is that we focus on ourselves more than our opponent. We run the same six or seven plays out of our base set every year. In an era, when everyone is changing offenses every year, we have been able to continue our success in the execution of our plays because of a commitment to our offense long term.

What piece of advice would you give to a head coach who wants to win a state championship?

My advice to young and upcoming head coaches is to understand leadership is from the top down; just because someone is the head coach does not mean he doesn't have to do the work that he did as an assistant coach. Understand this game is about relationships, too—not just wins and losses.

What do you consider the one most important aspect of your championship team this year? How did you develop that in your program?

The most important aspect of us winning championships is our commitment to consistency. We sell to our kids that winning in football comes from sticking with your system and understanding Chuck Knoll's quote: "Champions don't beat themselves; they just do the ordinary things better than their opponent day in and day out."

Georgia Division A

Coach: Donald Chumley

School: Savannah Christian High School

City: Savannah

2011 Record: 15-0, 5-0

Championship Game Results:

Savannah Christian	20
Landmark Christian (Fairburn)	3

State Championships at School: 1

Years as Head Coach: 7

Years at Current School: 7

State Championships Won as Head Coach: 1

What did you do differently this year from the other programs in your league, your section, your state that enabled your success as a state champion?

What piece of advice would you give to a head coach who wants to win a state championship?

What do you consider the one most important aspect of your championship team this year? How did you develop that in your program?

At Savannah Christian, we prepare each workout, each practice, and each day for games 11 through 15. It is on the weight room wall, it is on every t-shirt, it is on every handout the kids receive year-round. We may not reach game 15 each year, but it is our goal. We set our goals high, and we talk about them year-round. We want our kids to dream and shoot for the moon, and just maybe they will grab a star.

Georgia GISA AAA

Coach: Barney Hester

School: Tattnall Square Academy

City: Macon

2011 Record: 11-2, 6-0

Championship Game Results:

Tattnall Square Academy	35
Stratford Academy (Macon)	12

State Championships at School: 11

Years as Head Coach: 37

Years at Current School: 30

State Championships Won as Head Coach: 11

What did you do differently this year from the other programs in your league, your section, your state that enabled your success as a state champion?

I'm not sure what the other teams did. We really didn't do anything differently than what we normally do. We expect to win each year and plan accordingly. The off-season program is where it all begins and where we put a lot of emphasis.

What piece of advice would you give to a head coach who wants to win a state championship?

Find an offensive and defensive system that you are comfortable with, and stay with it. We have run an I formation option offense and a 52 (3-4) defense for 30 years. Our kids know and understand the system. Another thing that makes a difference is playing as many players as you can, whether as starters on offense or defense, or as starters on a special team.

What do you consider the one most important aspect of your championship team this year? How did you develop that in your program?

Our team unity was outstanding. It started with our seniors and filtered through all the classes. We have been very blessed over last 30 years, winning the state championship 11 times and playing for the title seven more times. The main ingredient of those teams was unity.

Idaho Division 2A

Coach: Jeff Lindsley

School: Grangeville High School

City: Grangeville

2011 Record: 12-0, 4-0

Championship Game Results:

Grangeville	36
Firth	6

State Championships at School: 1

Years as Head Coach: 2

Years at Current School: 6

State Championships Won as Head Coach: 1

What did you do differently this year from the other programs in your league, your section, your state that enabled your success as a state champion?

As far as doing anything differently, this year as a staff, we were better at practice planning and time allocation for all of our practices. We went to a clinic at Boise State, and it really opened our eyes on how to break away from a traditional football practice. Specifically, we tried not to have a period go over 8 to 10 minutes max. This allowed us to make sure we could rep more technique daily. At our level, we don't always have the prototypical kids in positions, so technique was absolutely huge for us. Great technique gave the kids added confidence against bigger/stronger opponents. We also tried to have at least three sessions in practice where we divided them up and held different types of contests where there was a clear winner and a clear loser, some contests that didn't have anything to do with football. Reinforcing how to win.

What piece of advice would you give to a head coach who wants to win a state championship?

All state playoff brackets are different each year. Some years, you're lucky to have a great team that is matched up with lesser teams. Still, that doesn't matter if you don't win your league in order to get there. We changed our approach from last year. We didn't even mention state when we started in August. That is too far into the future for high school–aged kids. Our basic concept was to measure how much we improved from Monday's practice to the end of our game on Friday night, which then served as our new starting point for the following Monday. Easier concept for the kids to grasp, and I don't think they felt that pressure that some programs place on their kids. It also gave them a constant metric that rewarded them for a hard week of practice.

What do you consider the one most important aspect of your championship team this year? How did you develop that in your program?

For our group, without question the most important aspect was that we had fun. In my opinion, kids these days are a little more sensitive from when I played. There is a fine line between fun and getting the hard, nasty work done in practice. As a staff, we agreed not to take ourselves too seriously, and the effect was less pressure on the kids. After all, while we still expect to win, this is still high school football. Our approach this next season will remain the same.

Personally, I like the hard-edged, sometimes brutal aspects of football, but I think that mentality is more appropriate at the higher levels of the game. In our area, most kids turn out for football as an opportunity to belong to an organized group of their friends, and to challenge themselves. Some are pushed by parents, others by peers. At the high school level, I still think football should be considered a game, and should be constructed that way until they start getting paid to play it; then, it's a profession. I've had the opportunity to coach as a grad assistant in college, and four years as an assistant high school coach here at Grangeville under two different head coaches. Between here and two different staffs at Boise State, I guess maybe I've seen enough different styles to compare against what we try to do here at Grangeville now.

Basically, as a staff, we try to keep the practices at as fast and high-energy as we can. We divide the kids up for competitions in practice that are not necessarily football-related, but give the kids a chance to laugh and challenge each other. Everything from lineman getting the chance to play wide receiver, tire pulls for bragging rights, and nicknames for most of the kids. We always try to monitor the attitude of the team, and when we see them starting to drag, we stop what we're doing, redirect, and then push to return to the pace we want. We joke around with the kids that need to be "brought back in the circle," rather than the typical yelling to get the required response we need. While we don't negotiate discipline, we do allow them a margin of levity that puts the responsibility on them to pull them out of the practice funk all kids experience from time to time. Bad practices always result in bad games on Friday night.

Idaho 1A Eight-Man

Coach: John Van Vliet

School: Lighthouse Christian High School

City: Twin Falls

2011 Record: 9-3, 4-2

Championship Game:

Lighthouse Christian	34
Carey	22

State Championships at School: 1

Years as Head Coach: 4

Years at Current School: 8

State Championships Won as Head Coach: 1

What did you do differently this year from the other programs in your league, your section, your state that enabled your success as a state champion?

I'm not sure what other programs do, but the thing we did differently within our own program was to commit to conditioning from the beginning of the season until the week of the championship. We did a good job conditioning guys in the past, but we felt we lost the commitment to it as the season progressed. I named a conditioning coach and promised to give him the time we needed. We never used conditioning for punitive purposes—only as a part of what we were trying to accomplish. As a 1A small school program, we ask our players to contribute a lot on the field. Many don't get an opportunity to come out of the game very often, so fitness is a key.

What piece of advice would you give to a head coach who wants to win a state championship?

My advice would be to focus on the game at hand and not to look too far forward.

What do you consider the one most important aspect of your championship team this year? How did you develop that in your program?

An important aspect of success was our "one body" philosophy. We stressed all year that there are many parts to a body, and that all are necessary and important. Everyone focused on their role and what they could do to help the entire body be stronger. We stressed that from the very beginning until the championship game.

Illinois Division 8A

Coach: John Ivlow

School: Bolingbrook High School

City: Bolingbrook

2011 Record: 13-1, 6-1

Championship Game Results:

Bolingbrook	21
Loyola	17

State Championships at School: 1

Years as Head Coach: 10

Years at Current School: 10

State Championships Won as Head Coach: 1

What did you do differently this year from the other programs in your league, your section, your state that enabled your success as a state champion?

We have done nothing differently. We have been knocking on the door forever, it seems like. We stuck to our beliefs, the biggest one being a platoon system. 45 out of 65 kids played in the state championship game. By doing this, we have developed more kids that are able to contribute. Individual improvement is the name of the game. We get better as the season goes on.

What piece of advice would you give to a head coach who wants to win a state championship?

Less is more. Some guys have play cards that look like they're from a cheap family restaurant. We have eight running plays, two play-action passes, and five three-step passes. Find what you believe in, and get good at it.

What do you consider the one most important aspect of your championship team this year? How did you develop that in your program?

The most important aspect of our program is our strength program. We lift weights throughout the off-season, summer, and in-season. We probably lift as much as we practice. We had two injures out of 65 guys over a 14-game season. Those two guys only missed a combined four games.

We check our egos at the door. We're all in this together at Bolingbrook High School.

Illinois Division 5A

Coach: Chris Andriano

School: Montini High School

City: Lombard

2011 Record: 12-2, 4-1

Championship Game Results:

Montini	70
Joliet Catholic Academy	45

State Championships at School: 4

Years as Head Coach: 33

Years at Current School: 33

State Championships Won as Head Coach: 4

What did you do differently this year from the other programs in your league, your section, your state that enabled your success as a state champion?

We first develop a culture of mental toughness and team unity in our off-season weights and conditioning program. It is very demanding and required for all players that are not out for a school sports team in the winter and spring. I take attendance every day and give positive feedback to every player. It really builds a team-first mentality. It all starts in the off-season for us.

What piece of advice would you give to a head coach who wants to win a state championship?

Be organized in every aspect of your program. From practice to team meetings and everything in between. I believe in making practice competitive. It puts pressure on players to perform and holds them accountable to do their best. We compete in drills as well as team scrimmages. This also puts a game-like pace to all of our practice segments.

What do you consider the one most important aspect of your championship team this year? How did you develop that in your program?

Mental toughness. We pride ourselves in a never-give-in, never-give-up, and never-say-die attitude with our program. We never show bad body language in any situation at any time in practice or games. Negative body language is an excuse for not getting the job done or is telling the other team and everyone in the stands that your will has been broken. That just can't ever happen. Our whole coaching staff harps on this in practice every day. I talk about this all the time in different ways.

Indiana Class 3A

Coach: Vincent Lorenzano

School: Bishop Chatard High School

City: Indianapolis

2011 Record: 13-2, 3-1

Championship Game Results:

Bishop Chatard	21
St. Joseph's (South Bend)	7

State Championships at School: 11

Years as Head Coach: 22

Years at Current School: 11

State Championships Won as Head Coach: 5

What did you do differently this year from the other programs in your league, your section, your state that enabled your success as a state champion?

We never worry about winning championships. We only concern ourselves with three things:

- What is our attitude?
- What is our effort?
- Did we get better each week?

What piece of advice would you give to a head coach who wants to win a state championship?

Your players need to know where you stand. What are you willing to do? What would you be willing to sacrifice? Express your true concern for your players. If a young man is willing to go out and lay it on the line for you, you better love them to death. Football is one of the last team sports where players can make ultimate sacrifices. Players need to know that you care. Are you a life-changer as a coach? You can be. Get your players to play to their potential by reaching down into their souls and pulling out everything that they have. Leave nothing on the table. Tell them the truth. If they lack effort, tell them. If practice is poor, tell them. Be honest and forthright. Get rid of your personal agenda. Everybody wants to win. All coaches are driven to succeed. It is those coaches who have eliminated their need to win and who focus on the molding of championship people that end up succeeding.

What do you consider the one most important aspect of your championship team this year? How did you develop that in your program?

They were consistent always and had a great sense of humor. They loved playing, and they loved the game of football. They played for a higher power than themselves.

Indiana Class AA

Coach: Matt Lindsay

School: Bishop Luers High School

City: Fort Wayne

2011 Record: 13-1, 6-1

Championship Game Results:

    Bishop Luers   41
    Mater Dei (Evansville)   17

State Championships at School: 10

Years as Head Coach: 25

Years at Current School: 25

State Championships Won as Head Coach: 9

What did you do differently this year from the other programs in your league, your section, your state that enabled your success as a state champion?

I don't know if we did anything different this year. We had great talent that came together. We have great pride in our program and the history and tradition of it that now includes 10 state champions. We stress to each class to work toward a positive legacy that they can leave behind.

What piece of advice would you give to a head coach who wants to win a state championship?

If I, as the head coach, have done anything successfully, one thing is to coach to your strengths. I have never been totally sold on one system that we insist on kids fitting that system. The talents of our kids dictate what our offensive and defensive philosophy is for that group of kids. It does change from one class of kids to another, and from decade to decade.

What do you consider the one most important aspect of your championship team this year? How did you develop that in your program?

Another key component of this year's team is the contributions of our young coaches. The veteran coaches turned over much of their responsibilities the past two years to their younger coaches, who we have been mentoring. Many of these young men are former Luers players. It was a joy to watch them be successful, energetic, and creative. We know the day will come when many of us (there are about six of us who have been together 20 plus years) will step aside. We can see that the future is already in good hands. Once again, the tradition factor is huge in our program.

Indiana Class 5A

Coach: Kevin Wright

School: Carmel High School

City: Carmel

2011 Record: 14-1, 7-1

Championship Game Results:

Carmel   54
Penn (Mishawaka) 0

State Championships at School: 7

Years as Head Coach: 18

Years at Current School: 2

State Championships Won as Head Coach: 4

Noteworthy: After the 2011 season, Carmel High School was ranked #1 in the state.

What did you do differently this year from the other programs in your league, your section, your state that enabled your success as a state champion?

I am not sure exactly what we do different than other teams in our state, but I do know that we have a 12-month program that we use to ensure we are doing something every day as coaches and players to improve. We break those 12 months up into pre-season, season, and post-season, and we have specific goals that we want to accomplish during each of those periods. We use the old philosophy regarding "Plan your work, then work your plan," and everybody in our program has bought into this approach.

What piece of advice would you give to a head coach who wants to win a state championship?

My best advice would be the same advice I would give to a first-year head coach, and that would be the only thing guaranteed concerning your next football season is that you are going to have adversity. So plan for it, and understand that your ultimate success is going to depend on how you deal with whatever adversity comes your way. Championship teams always seem to find a way to overcome obstacles. That is why at each end of our locker room we have a sign that reads: "No Excuses: Win the Day."

What do you consider the one most important aspect of your championship team this year? How did you develop that in your program?

I think the most important characteristic of our team this year was resiliency. For us, that started with tremendous leadership from our senior class. We were not the most physically talented team in the state, but we played extremely hard, we played very smart, and we played very unselfishly together. In the playoffs, we were behind twice by three scores at the half, yet kept our poise and found a way to win the game. Our coaches and players were resilient, never panicked, and believed in each other no matter what we encountered. It takes talent to win a championship, but there are a lot of very talented teams that never come close because they lack some of the characteristics I just mentioned. This was a very special team, one that both our school and community are very proud of and won't soon be forgotten.

Indiana Class 4A

Coach: Rick Streiff

School: Cathedral High School

City: Indianapolis

2011 Record: 12-3 (freelance, no league standings)

Championship Game Results:

Cathedral	42
Washington (South Bend)	7

State Championships at School: 9

Years as Head Coach: 24

Years at Current School: 17

State Championships Won as Head Coach: 7

What did you do differently this year from the other programs in your league, your section, your state that enabled your success as a state champion?

We do not do anything differently. Our players have had some success, and we believe our success breeds success. We speak to our players about what will be their legacy in our program. We speak to them about what they owe to those who went before them.

What piece of advice would you give to a head coach who wants to win a state championship?

Focus on the little things. This is the best piece of advice I ever received as a coach. Take care of the small things that are important (fundamentals, relationships between teammates and coaches), and the big things like winning will come. Be committed to your values, and stick with them, even if it costs you games now, because you will win in the future.

What do you consider the one most important aspect of your championship team this year? How did you develop that in your program?

"Brotherhood is everything" is our constant motto. We believe that by creating relationships between players and players and coaches that a level of trust results that makes teams fight through the tough times.

We create tough times during practice where the players have to count on each other. What is learned is that you must be counted on in order to count on others.

Iowa Division 4A

Coach: Gary Swenson

School: Valley High School

City: West Des Moines

2011 Record: 14-0, 5-0

Championship Game Results:

    Valley   17
    Bettendorf 14

State Championships at School: 5

Years as Head Coach: 38

Years at Current School: 17

State Championships Won as Head Coach: 6

What did you do differently this year from the other programs in your league, your section, your state that enabled your success as a state champion?

We did not do anything differently this past year than any other year. It takes talent, depth, and coaches that can teach the game to win a state championship. All of the teams in our league are well-coached. We were fortunate to keep all of our key players healthy this past season. In game 14, which was our state championship game, we had the same starting lineup we had in game one. All of our players had made dramatic improvement throughout the season.

What piece of advice would you give to a head coach who wants to win a state championship?

All coaches want to win a state championship. My advice would be to have a plan, and work as hard as possible to execute that plan. Be genuine, honest, and consistent with your players and coaches. Be sure everyone knows what your expectations are in all areas of your program. Be straightforward and concise in your communication with parents. Explain in great detail to parents and players how you determine playing time. Lay out in clear detail rules and regulations that make sense and are easy to understand. Be sure your coaches can teach the game. Keep things simple for your players so they can play fast. Be relentless in teaching the fundamentals of the game.

What do you consider the one most important aspect of your championship team this year? How did you develop that in your program?

We base our program on winning. Winning in the classroom, winning on and off the field. I think this past year we were able to embrace the big game and the opportunity it gave us to compete and beat the best our schedule had to offer. We try to develop the knowledge with our players and coaches that all we can do is the best we can. If our best isn't good enough, then we will credit our opponent with a job well done.

Kansas 2 1A

Coach: Larry Glatczak

School: Centralia/Wetmore High School

City: Centralia

2011 Record: 10-3, 3-0

Championship Game Results:

Centralia/Wetmore	20 (in overtime)
La Crosse	14

State Championships at School: 2

Years as Head Coach: 7

Years at Current School: 7

State Championships Won as Head Coach: 2

What did you do differently this year from the other programs in your league, your section, your state that enabled your success as a state champion?

We focus on the little things in football. We run the single-wing offense and really pay attention to detail and executing the plays to perfection. We also play a very tough non-conference schedule in weeks 1 through 3. I really believe that has been a success for us. In 2009, when we won a state championship, we got beat the first week and made changes to our defense that enabled us to become a better team defensively. This year was no different. We started the season 1-3, playing one and two classes above us. From that, we made changes to our team and ended with a championship.

What piece of advice would you give to a head coach who wants to win a state championship?

Don't get too fancy with the offense and defense. It's like the KISS method: keep it simple, stupid. Some coaches want to run 10 different offenses and defenses, and the kids are so confused they can't execute anything. The second thing is to show respect to the players. We at Centralia feel we have a great relationship with the players. Our coaching staff gives respect to the kids, and in return we get it back. I think that is so important in a team. They will run through a brick wall for us; in turn, we will do anything to help our kids.

What do you consider the one most important aspect of your championship team this year? How did you develop that in your program?

The one important aspect this year was trust. We had nine seniors that came together around week 5 and got better and better as the season went. By the playoffs, our kids trusted each other and had a ton of confidence. Take one game at a time, and don't let the outside sources impede with what the team wants to accomplish. Stay focused and most importantly have fun.

Kansas Division 5A

Coach: Randy Dreiling

School: Hutchinson High School

City: Hutchinson

2011 Record: 11-2, 5-0

Championship Game Results:

| Hutchinson | 33 |
| Blue Valley (Stillwell) | 21 |

State Championships at School: 7

Years as Head Coach: 22

Years at Current School: 15

State Championships Won as Head Coach: 7

What did you do differently this year from the other programs in your league, your section, your state that enabled your success as a state champion?

What piece of advice would you give to a head coach who wants to win a state championship?

What do you consider the one most important aspect of your championship team this year? How did you develop that in your program?

We believe a program needs an identity to be successful. We build ours in the weight room the entire year.

Kansas 6A

Coach: Jeff Gourley

School: Olathe South High School

City: Olathe

2011 Record: 12-1, 7-0

Championship Game Results:

    Olathe   41
    Heights (Wichita) 37

State Championships at School: 1

Years as Head Coach: 22

Years at Current School: 4

State Championships Won as Head Coach: 1

What did you do differently this year from the other programs in your league, your section, your state that enabled your success as a state champion?

I really can't say what we did differently than other teams. In order to identify differences, I would need to know what others are doing, which I don't. Due to the previous thought, I will only be able to speculate as to what we did differently than other programs.

At Olathe South, we pride ourselves on discipline across the board. Like other schools, discipline is expected on the field, around the locker room, and all areas related to football. A possible difference between other schools and us may be the extra expectations we put on our players. While our coaches provide constant guidance and support, we expect our players to discipline themselves in the classroom, hallways, lunchroom, and at home or other social events outside of the school. We require our players to utilize conversation tactics that acknowledge their subservient role in the educational setting. If all of this sounds strange, let me explain in simple terms.

We require our players to respond to teachers and coaches, or any adult, with "Yes, sir" or "Yes, ma'am" and "No, sir" or "No, ma'am." This may sound silly, but it demonstrates respect and puts the players in a mindset of being the learner, not the teacher. When this mentality is practiced in the classroom daily, then it comes onto the field for practice. At that point, we are able to teach the things necessary to be successful on game nights without players questioning the reason. Learning happens much quicker.

We express to parents our emphasis for discipline at our first meeting. We explain that discipline is something we do for the player, not to the player.

What piece of advice would you give to a head coach who wants to win a state championship?

I would assume every coach wants to win a state championship, but they also need to understand there isn't a perfect system, a definite blueprint, or any other magic pill for a program to achieve success. Coaches should research all aspects of football, decide on their philosophical approach, and then implement a plan. Once the plan is deemed to be fundamentally solid, stick to it. Coaches that waffle will rarely achieve long-term success.

In short, do what you believe, and believe what you do. It is fine to tweak systems to fit personnel, but stay within the parameters of your basic philosophy.

What do you consider the one most important aspect of your championship team this year? How did you develop that in your program?

Team chemistry has been a critical component of every successful team I have coached. Without a "we are all in this together" mentality, teams have a tendency to break apart during the rough parts of a season, and all seasons have rough parts. We attempt to build team chemistry through the off-season. The old saying "Misery loves company" comes into play during our off-season program. We really stress the fact that everyone is working hard to achieve the same goal; everyone is making sacrifices to be good; everyone is paying the same price for success. If we can get that message into our players' heads, we normally have a very good season.

Let's not fool ourselves, though. Talent is the main factor to winning state championships. If your team has talent and the willingness to work as a single unit, success will come.

Kentucky Division 5A

Coach: Kevin Wallace

School: Bowling Green High School

City: Bowling Green

2011 Record: 15-0, 4-0

Championship Game Results:

| Bowling Green | 55 |
| Anderson County (Lawrenceburg) | 3 |

State Championships at School: 2

Years as Head Coach: 26

Years at Current School: 16

State Championships Won as Head Coach: 1

What did you do differently this year from the other programs in your league, your section, your state that enabled your success as a state champion?

In all honesty, I do not know what other programs do on a daily basis, so it is difficult for me to say how we differed from other programs in our class. We are blessed to have an talented, experienced staff who has been together for a long period of time, great facilities and support from our administration and community, and most importantly, talented players who were willing to place team success ahead of their individual aspirations.

What piece of advice would you give to a head coach who wants to win a state championship?

Cultivate an atmosphere that allows all the important parts of a program feel that they have ownership in the success or failure of that program. This would include anyone that touches your program on a daily basis. Make certain all your administrators, coaches, players, trainers, bus drivers, custodial staff, etc. feel like they are working with you, not for you.

What do you consider the one most important aspect of your championship team this year? How did you develop that in your program?

The chemistry of a team is developed in the months of training that lead to a season. The leadership of our coaches and seniors established a great foundation for our team as we worked in the winter months. The work ethic that results from our training in the off-season has been a core of our success for many years. It allows our players to push each other to new competitive standards and develop a toughness level that will allow them to conquer the adversities that a season brings.

Kentucky 4A

Coach: Dale Mueller

School: Highlands High School

City: Fort Thomas

2011 Record: 15-0, 4-0

Championship Game Results:

| Highlands | 42 |
| Franklin-Simpson | 14 |

State Championships at School: 21

Years as Head Coach: 27

Years at Current School: 18

State Championships Won as Head Coach: 10

What did you do differently this year from the other programs in your league, your section, your state that enabled your success as a state champion?

What piece of advice would you give to a head coach who wants to win a state championship?

What do you consider the one most important aspect of your championship team this year? How did you develop that in your program?

The biggest thing we do differently is that, every day throughout the year, it is important to us to develop as football players and as men. We try harder on a year-round basis because it means a lot to us.

Follow-up question: Would you mind giving me three or ways in which you do that because I think so many coaches are into the X's and O's part, this would be great info for them to have, something for them to think about?

Okay. We are 73-2 and have won the state championship the last five years, not because we know something that others don't or have some unique scheme. We do believe in our schemes. We are a high-speed offense that snaps the ball as soon as the official sets the ball. We are a complete two-platoon team, although we are a public school with only 400 boys in the school. We will have 160 of them out for football. All the coaches are speed and strength coaches, and they all work with our players year-round. Our players try harder on a year-round basis than players at other schools. If anything but that last sentence is emphasized, then my message on how to be a consistent state champion is missed.

Kentucky Division 2A

Coach: Bruce Kozerski

School: Holy Cross High School

City: Covington

2011 Record: 12-3, 3-1

Championship Game Results:

Holy Cross	33
Glasgow (Greenwood)	14

State Championships at School: 1

Years as Head Coach: 8

Years at Current School: 8

State Championships Won as Head Coach: 1

What did you do differently this year from the other programs in your league, your section, your state that enabled your success as a state champion?

We spread the field with talented receivers and made the defense defend 53 yards wide by 50 yards deep. By spreading the field, we make the defenders play in space. Pass protection must be flexible enough either through blocking scheme or by route breakoff to keep the defense off of your quarterback.

What piece of advice would you give to a head coach who wants to win a state championship?

I would advise any coach to fix your team's performance one play at a time. Block and tackle your opponents, yes, but typically poor performances are a result of individuals not fixing the details of their position. If you can fix your own technique weakness, you will expose the weakness of your opponents.

What do you consider the one most important aspect of your championship team this year? How did you develop that in your program?

Confidence. We fixed so many issues we had with our own fundamentals that one win after another, our confidence grew, and we really began to believe in what we were doing. We got it right at the right time. We learned about ourselves early in the season and fixed us. This is developed through hard work and continued positive reinforcement of good play performances.

Louisiana Division 4A

Coach: Mickey McCarty

School: Neville High School

City: Monroe

2011 Record: 14-0, 4-0

Championship Game Results:

Neville High	27
Karr (New Orleans)	6

State Championships at School: 2

Years as Head Coach: 10

Years at Current School: 10

State Championships Won as Head Coach: 2

What did you do differently this year from the other programs in your league, your section, your state that enabled your success as a state champion?

What piece of advice would you give to a head coach who wants to win a state championship?

What do you consider the one most important aspect of your championship team this year? How did you develop that in your program?

One change we had this year different from past seasons was an in-season lifting program that was unlike any we had tried before. We felt that we were better prepared physically unlike any year in the past. This was essential every game, but evident as a difference-maker throughout the playoffs. Other than that, no secrets here. We had a quality group of athletes and young men, a hard-working group of coaches, a school and community full of supporters, a plan of action, and we all got in the same boat and rowed the same direction. I have been a part of good teams with individuals who wanted to row the boat a different direction, and that can destroy the mission. We were blessed this year. 14-0. School's 10th state championship, and we were sure proud to continue the great tradition here.

Maine Division C

Coach: Jim Hartman

School: Yarmouth High School

City: Yarmouth

2011 Record: 12-0, 6-0

Championship Game Results:

| Yarmouth | 41 |
| Bucksport | 14 |

State Championships at School: 2

Years as Head Coach: 5

Years at Current School: 5

State Championships Won as Head Coach: 2

What did you do differently this year from the other programs in your league, your section, your state that enabled your success as a state champion?

I think the biggest difference for us was the attitude of the program. Not just from the players but everyone in the program. The program established the goal of winning our second championship in a row, and it was the focus of all that we did. We all believed!

Every lift in the weight room, every lap and every rep in practice, every fundraiser, and every meal for the team was about being a champion. Everyone also believed that we were going to be champions. Therefore, practice, games, booster meetings, and everything else had a meaning.

We were, I believe, the best-conditioned team, allowing us persevere when our opponents wilted late in the game. Our players were the most determined team.

What piece of advice would you give to a head coach who wants to win a state championship?

If you want to be a champion, I believe you must believe. This is the first requirement. You also must be the best-conditioned team and stress fundamentals. Players must have a complete and thorough knowledge of your system. You must believe in your team and them in you.

What do you consider the one most important aspect of your championship team this year? How did you develop that in your program?

Belief in each other, the system, and the goal. Absolutely the difference. I think that in order to develop that belief, we just walked it, preached it, and lived it. With positive attitudes from everyone involved. We do not allow a negative thought to be spoken or acted upon. Using the word "can't" is immediate laps.

Maryland MIAA Division B

Coach: Ken Lucas

School: Annapolis Area Christian School

City: Severn

2011 Record: 10-2, 5-1

Championship Game Results:

Annapolis Area Christian	46
Boys Latin (Baltimore)	13

State Championships at School: 3

Years as Head Coach: 13

Years at Current School: 5

State Championships Won as Head Coach: 4

What did you do differently this year from the other programs in your league, your section, your state that enabled your success as a state champion?

Not sure what we did differently; however, I know as a staff, we felt we had to take care of us first. We felt that we had the talent and capabilities to be successful; however, we felt strongly that we needed to work hard on team chemistry. By creating a family-like environment and brotherhood amongst the players, we felt strongly that success was possible. Naturally, we would have to make plays as well; however, playing "together" would certainly optimize those opportunities.

What piece of advice would you give to a head coach who wants to win a state championship?

If I had a perfect remedy for winning state championships, I would bottle it and sell it. Certainly, you need players to win championships. You also need dedication and sacrifice from the staff, players, families, and the school community. I believe championships are won as a community. The support, belief, and hard work by all culminates into good things.

What do you consider the one most important aspect of your championship team this year? How did you develop that in your program?

Team unity and faith as one unit. Our team believed that it was possible to win. Belief doesn't always do it alone; however, it's a good start. I'm not talking about being cocky or overconfident; I'm merely talking about working hard and believing in each other's ability within that team. We preached team unity and practiced team unity. I believe team unity is a big part of team success.

Maryland Division 2A

Coach: Kevin Lynott

School: Middletown High School

City: Middletown

2011 Record: 13-1, 7-1

Championship Game Results:

Middletown	43
Douglass (Upper Marlboro)	6

State Championships at School: 1

Years as Head Coach: 4

Years at Current School: 4

State Championships Won as Head Coach: 1

What did you do differently this year from the other programs in your league, your section, your state that enabled your success as a state champion?

We have a great feeder program (K-8) with the MVAA League. We have a great strength and conditioning program and instructor with Coach Lorne Ridenour. We have a true team approach in our leadership as coaches and players.

What piece of advice would you give to a head coach who wants to win a state championship?

Study the successful programs in your area and around the country. Success leaves clues: being willing to put quality time into your program, keeping a balanced life with your family, not sacrificing your family for football. Faith, family, job, football.

What do you consider the one most important aspect of your championship team this year? How did you develop that in your program?

Team-first attitude, unselfish attitude model by coaches, talented players.

Massachusetts Division C2

Coach: Ken Tucker

School: Nashoba Regional High School

City: Bolton

2011 Record: 13-0, 5-0

Championship Game Results:

| Nashoba Regional | 27 |
| Holy Name Central Catholic (Worcester) | 0 |

State Championships at School: 2

Years as Head Coach: 24

Years at Current School: 24

State Championships Won as Head Coach: 2

What did you do differently this year from the other programs in your league, your section, your state that enabled your success as a state champion?

What piece of advice would you give to a head coach who wants to win a state championship?

What do you consider the one most important aspect of your championship team this year? How did you develop that in your program?

At Nashoba Regional, we take pride in the history of our program. We celebrated our 50th year as a school and football program this past season. Our success for 2011 began with the disappointing ending to our 2010 season, when we lost a tough game that few gave us a chance to win. Our players and coaches used this as motivation to be better in 2011. Off-season was obviously a key, as was our focus on leadership and taking one game at a time. We knew we would have to be ready right out of the gate, facing a tough season opener and early season schedule. As a result, we set up our pre-season to challenge ourselves to be the best. We scrimmaged teams that all ended up reaching championship games, as it turned out. Our readiness for the start of the season and our ability to play one game at a time while focusing on improving fundamentally each week were key. Our team leaders set a positive example. We retained our focus. Individual players had great seasons, but all realized that our success would be the result of a true team effort, and all were willing to do whatever it took to win.

Michigan Eight-Man

Coach: Tim Brabant

School: Carsonville-Port Sanilac High School

City: Carsonville

2011 Record: 12-1, 5-1

Championship Game Results:

| Carsonville-Port Sanilac | 59 |
| Rapid River | 20 |

State Championships at School: 2

Years as Head Coach: 2

Years at Current School: 2

State Championships Won as Head Coach: 2

Noteworthy: Coach Brabant won state championships in each of his first two seasons as head coach.

What did you do differently this year from the other programs in your league, your section, your state that enabled your success as a state champion?

What separated us from the rest of the teams was or commitment to our off-season strength and conditioning program. We had 100 percent commitment two hours per day, five days a week for the entire summer. Our players were much stronger, faster, and polished than the players on the other teams we played. Our ability to maintain our focus and efforts on our team philosophy of: one rep, one day, one team, and one week at a time really gave us the psychological edge on our opponents throughout the season.

What piece of advice would you give to a head coach who wants to win a state championship?

If you want to win a state championship, you have to get the players bought into you as much as the program. They have to be willing to sacrifice themselves for the success of the team. They have to believe and honor the fact that they owe their time and dedication to the team, the school, their parents, and the community. They also have to know that you are willing to make the same commitment.

What do you consider the one most important aspect of your championship team this year? How did you develop that in your program?

The most important aspect to this year's team was phenomenal work ethic, character, and athleticism. We had a group of seniors who refused to be outworked or outplayed each and every week. You cannot win unless your kids are 100 percent committed year-round. For instance, our kids don't drink pop. Speed, strength, and proper rest and nutrition are the three pieces of the triangle we focus on most. Have your kids play as much football as they can in the summer, 7-on-7s, attend one to two team camps, and have the seniors set up some captain's practices. Don't make your kids feel like they're locked in a position like a robot. Teach them to think for themselves so that they do not have to think at all on the field. Offensively, you have to save things for the tournament. Defensively you have to be willing to adjust, and always be flexible. They work our speed training regularly and lift with excitement.

Michigan Division 6

Coach: Terry Hessbrook

School: Ithaca High School

City: Ithaca

2011 Record: 14-0, 7-0

Championship Game Results:

Ithaca	42
Constantine	0

State Championships at School: 2

Years as Head Coach: 8

Years at Current School: 16

State Championships Won as Head Coach: 2

Noteworthy: Ithaca High School was the Division 6 State Champion with a 14-0 record in 2010, 2011, and 2012. This garnered the school the longest active winning streak (42) in the state of Michigan in all divisions.

What did you do differently this year from the other programs in your league, your section, your state that enabled your success as a state champion?

What piece of advice would you give to a head coach who wants to win a state championship?

What do you consider the one most important aspect of your championship team this year? How did you develop that in your program?

Our approach is very simple. We try to outwork every team that we are going to play in every aspect of the game: weight room, summer conditioning, practices, preparation, games—everything. We know that this is not an easy goal to measure. It is, however, something that we do have direct control over.

Michigan Division 8

Coach: John Schwartz

School: Mendon High School

City: Mendon

2011 Record: 14-0, 3-0

Championship Game Results:

| Mendon | 33 |
| Fowler | 0 |

State Championships at School: 11

Years as Head Coach: 23

Years at Current School: 23

State Championships Won as Head Coach: 10

What did you do differently this year from the other programs in your league, your section, your state that enabled your success as a state champion?

We do the same thing year after year, and we don't change much. Our fifth and sixth graders run the same drills and use the same terminology as our kids. Our JV practice with our varsity and learn from our older kids. Our summer program keeps our kids together and is a big part of our team unity.

What piece of advice would you give to a head coach who wants to win a state championship?

You never know enough. Talk to and ask questions of other coaches, high school and college. X's and O's don't win games; kids do. Get them in their correct positions, teach them, and get them to work together.

What do you consider the one most important aspect of your championship team this year? How did you develop that in your program?

The leadership from our captains and seniors this year was awesome. Developing leaders started years before their senior year. Looking back at old team pictures, our strongest captains were managers as fifth and sixth graders.

Michigan Division 7

Coach: Mike Boyd

School: Nouvel Catholic Central High School

City: Saginaw

2011 Record: 13-0, 2-0

Championship Game Results:

Nouvel Catholic Central	56
Pewamo-Westphalia	26

State Championships at School: 3

Years as Head Coach: 13

Years at Current School: 13

State Championships Won as Head Coach: 3

What did you do differently this year from the other programs in your league, your section, your state that enabled your success as a state champion?

We always like to challenge our kids, and we had a special challenge for them this year. Our senior class is a very talented class that had essentially underachieved. This was their challenge: to prove they were more than just a group of talented individuals. They were challenged to prove they were also mentally and physically tough. The previous season, they had demonstrated the inability to deal with in-game adversity, and so we focused on developing that mental toughness and trust in one another.

What piece of advice would you give to a head coach who wants to win a state championship?

Not to focus on winning a state championship. If it's meant to be, it will happen. Focus on developing your student athletes in all areas to prepare them to be successful in life.

What do you consider the one most important aspect of your championship team this year? How did you develop that in your program?

We have a very unique training camp right before the season that develops team unity, leadership, and mental toughness, along with focusing on our core values of faith, family, character, and attitude. We train on sand dunes, ski slopes, and trails, and we have team-building exercises. Our seniors took charge from the beginning and made it our most successful camp to date. Their leadership and attention to detail was tremendous, and it carried us throughout the season.

Minnesota Class 2A

Coach: Brent Schroeder

School: Caledonia High School

City: Caledonia

2011 Record: 13-1, 5-0

Championship Game Results:

> Calendonia   27
> Moose Lake/Willow River   0

State Championships at School: 5

Years as Head Coach: 2

Years at Current School: 2

State Championships Won as Head Coach: 2

Noteworthy: Coach Schroeder's team won back-to-back state championships in his first two years as head coach.

What did you do differently this year from the other programs in your league, your section, your state that enabled your success as a state champion?

We have been very blessed to win state the last four out of five years. As a staff, we probably preach and teach rest and recovery more than any other team in the state. Our kids continue to grow stronger and faster as the season goes on. It is all about being healthy in the end.

What piece of advice would you give to a head coach who wants to win a state championship?

You cannot win unless your kids are 100 percent committed year-round. For instance, our kids don't drink pop. Speed, strength, and proper rest and nutrition are the three pieces of the triangle we focus on most. Have your kids play as much football as they can in the summer, 7-on-7s, attend one to two team camps, and have the seniors set up some captains practices. Don't make your kids feel like they're locked in a position like a robot. Teach them to think for themselves so that they do not have to think at all on the field. Offensively, you have to save things for the tournament. Defensively, you have to be willing to adjust, and always be flexible. They work our speed training regularly and lift with excitement

What do you consider the one most important aspect of your championship team this year? How did you develop that in your program?

Leadership and excitement. It's your team—take it wherever you want.

Minnesota Class 4A

Coach: Mike Rowe

School: Rocori High School

City: Cold Spring

2011 Record: 12-1, 5-1

Championship Game Results:

> Rocori   17
> Bemidji   10

State Championships at School: 1

Years as Head Coach: 4

Years at Current School: 3

State Championships Won as Head Coach: 1

What did you do differently this year from the other programs in your league, your section, your state that enabled your success as a state champion?

What piece of advice would you give to a head coach who wants to win a state championship?

What do you consider the one most important aspect of your championship team this year? How did you develop that in your program?

The advice I would give a coach is don't coach football just to be a champion. Your job as a coach is to teach your athletes how to become better people in society. If you are coaching to win, you are in it for the wrong reasons.

This season we chose to concentrate on three specific things. The first thing we did is get our kids to buy into the importance of the weight room all summer long. The next thing we did was teach our kids to compete every day no matter what the situation was. The last thing we did was teach character because everything is easy when you are winning. Your true character comes out in times of adversity. Every player needed to attend our Monday meeting, where we introduced a new character topic each week.

Minnesota Division AAA

Coach: Carl Lemke

School: St. Croix Lutheran High School

City: West St. Paul

2011 Record: 14-0, 8-0

Championship Game Results:

| St. Croix Lutheran | 34 |
| Fairmont | 32 |

State Championships at School: 1

Years as Head Coach: 39

Years at Current School: 17

State Championships Won as Head Coach: 4

What did you do differently this year from the other programs in your league, your section, your state that enabled your success as a state champion?

Sorry. I do not know enough about other programs.

What piece of advice would you give to a head coach who wants to win a state championship?

Get a system you like, and stick with it. Work hard to improve the details of that system. Do not jump around, adding aspects to a system that may look good to start with. Consistency in a system for grades 9 through 12 is vital.

What do you consider the one most important aspect of your championship team this year? How did you develop that in your program?

Athletes carried out each assignment to a high degree of excellence. It is developed through consistency and repetition.

Missouri Division 6

Coach: Greg Oder

School: Blue Springs South High School

City: Blue Springs

2011 Record: 12-2, 4-1

Championship Game Results:

Blue Springs	40
Christian Brothers (St. Louis)	37

State Championships at School: 2

Years as Head Coach: 11

Years at Current School: 20

State Championships Won as Head Coach: 2

What did you do differently this year from the other programs in your league, your section, your state that enabled your success as a state champion?

The most important part of our team this year was the fact that our team was selfless. They were a very close-knit group that didn't care who got the credit; they just wanted to win. You have to find a way to get that through to your athletes. The team will be much better without individuals.

What piece of advice would you give to a head coach who wants to win a state championship?

This is the first year that I can remember when we had good strong leadership in every position group. That is priceless. We work on that all summer long.

What do you consider the one most important aspect of your championship team this year? How did you develop that in your program?

I don't think you can go out and try to win the state championship from the beginning. It's about trying to make your group into the best team they can become. A state championship is too broad and too far away to worry about at the beginning of the season. But at the same time, your leaders have to believe that winning a state championship is feasible. That's why the first one, in my opinion, is the hardest. It takes a very special group to believe they can do something that nobody else has done. The coaching staff, obviously, plays a role in what the team believes.

Missouri Division 2

Coach: Scott Bailey

School: Lamar High School

City: Lamar

2011 Record: 14-1, 6-1

Championship Game:

Lamar	49
Lafayette County (Higginsville)	19

State Championships at School: 1

Years as Head Coach: 7

Years at Current School: 6

State Championships Won as Head Coach: 1

What did you do differently this year from the other programs in your league, your section, your state that enabled your success as a state champion?

No answer.

What piece of advice would you give to a head coach who wants to win a state championship?

Focus on what is important: the kids. Don't focus on what you don't have, or what your competition does have, or the people that say it can't be done. The kids are the reason we are here, and them making plays on game day is what will win a championship.

What do you consider the one most important aspect of your championship team this year? How did you develop that in your program?

I would say the belief in each other we call "brotherhood." It helped sustain us through our year-round strength and conditioning program, helped us overcome a week 6 loss in a big game environment, and made the process of building a football program more enjoyable—that and a large group of outstanding young men that are very good athletes that play very good football.

Missouri Division 5

Coach: Frederick Bouchard

School: Staley High School

City: Kansas City

2011 Record: 14-0, 5-0

Championship Game Results:

Staley   35
Kirkwood   21

State Championships at School: 1

Years as Head Coach: 19

Years at Current School: 4

State Championships Won as Head Coach: 5

Noteworthy: Staley High School won its first state championship just four years after the school opened.

What did you do differently this year from the other programs in your league, your section, your state that enabled your success as a state champion?

It rarely has to do with what we did this year, but rather what habits we established three or four years ago when these current seniors were in their freshman and sophomore years that paid huge dividends this season. Truthfully, I'm not sure what other folks do, but we have a system and structure in place that allows us to help our athletes grow as people, students, and athletes. We purposefully teach a character curriculum, and we think that part of our success is the character development we do with our players throughout the year. We work awfully hard in the weight room, on the practice field, and in the film room, too.

What piece of advice would you give to a head coach who wants to win a state championship?

Don't forget to teach beyond the game to your players. You may or may not win championships, but you will at least know you attempted to pour good stuff into your players when you had them. Also, remember to build your student leaders and provide them with skills to tackle the upcoming season. Also, work the weight room extremely hard on a year-round basis. If you work hard there, it will pay big dividends in a few years. That development doesn't happen overnight though and needs to time to mature.

What do you consider the one most important aspect of your championship team this year? How did you develop that in your program?

We had great leadership from our student-athletes. Whenever I've had great leadership on our team, our success followed. We do leadership training with our upcoming seniors, and we talk about using those skills regularly. Our senior group was on point, and they bought into that concept. We will continue to work on building our student leaders on a regular basis.

Missouri Eight-Man

Coach: Chuck Borey

School: Worth County High School

City: Grant City

2011 Record: 13-0, 8-0

Championship Game Results:

Worth County	50
Mound City	20

State Championships at School: 5

Years as Head Coach: 15

Years at Current School: 15

State Championships Won as Head Coach: 5

What did you do differently this year from the other programs in your league, your section, your state that enabled your success as a state champion?

What piece of advice would you give to a head coach who wants to win a state championship?

What do you consider the one most important aspect of your championship team this year? How did you develop that in your program?

We made sure that each player had a role and knew what their role on the team was. Also, as a head coach, I truly believe you will only be as good as your assistant coaches. If you surround yourself with good people, good things will happen. Last thing is to be open and true to your players; make sure they know where they stand and where you stand. This will give them the respect and willingness to go out every Friday night and bust theirs for the team.

Montana AA

Coach: Pat Murphy

School: Capital High School

City: Helena

2011 Record: 12-1, 9-1

Championship Game Results:

Capital	39
Billings West	14

State Championships at School: 11

Years as Head Coach: 18

Years at Current School: 9

State Championships Won as Head Coach: 4

What did you do differently this year from the other programs in your league, your section, your state that enabled your success as a state champion?

We have been to the state championship six of the last seven years, winning four titles. We are the third-smallest public school in a conference of 14. The thing I believe we do differently than other schools in our league is that we don't focus on the negatives, but concentrate on our positives. We could sit back and complain that we are a small school and we are playing schools with 1,000 more students than us. Instead, we use that as a positive. We tell our student-athletes we must work harder than other schools in order to be successful—and this starts in the weight room. We want our student-athletes to do all sports, and our coaches at our school agree and encourage their athletes go out for other activities. This is what sets our school apart from the others. In a time of traveling teams and specialization of sports, we are unified as coaches. We find, because of this, our kids are great competitors, and we win a lot of games in pressure situations. This is because they compete year-round. They have learned how to compete and play hard.

What piece of advice would you give to a head coach who wants to win a state championship?

We never talk about winning. Winning is a by-product of outexecuting and outworking your opponent. Focus on what you can control, which are the little things: footwork, technique and off-season training. We are always stressing to our student-athletes to not look at the score board, trust their teammates, and trust their coaches. Fans should be able to come to our games at anytime and not be able to tell if we are up by 42 or down by 42 points because of our level of play. Our level and intensity of play should be consistent no matter what the score. This attitude takes time to develop. You must constantly coach your athletes on footwork and doing things perfectly. You must develop an atmosphere in which the athlete is expected to go hard at every snap. Film study is an excellent way to get this done.

What do you consider the one most important aspect of your championship team this year? How did you develop that in your program?

The last piece of advice is to build relationships with your student-athletes. Find out what is going on in their lives, what are their interests, and find out what activities outside of football they are doing. And above all, be visible in their other activities. Go to their speech and debate meets; tell them they ran a good race in track. High-five those when they do well on their math test. When you develop these kind a relationships, they will play harder for you, they will respect you, and problems outside of football will be minimized.

Montana Six-Man

Coach: Scott Sparks

School: Denton High School

City: Denton

2011 Record: 12-0, 6-0

Championship Game Results:

> Denton   72
> Savage   30

State Championships at School: 3

Years as Head Coach: 7

Years at Current School: 2

State Championships Won as Head Coach: 2

What did you do differently this year from the other programs in your league, your section, your state that enabled your success as a state champion?

Our success was made in the weight room. The senior boys, from the time they were eighth graders, put the time in the summer and throughout the year to get bigger, faster, and stronger. I also felt like our kids played with a winning attitude, meaning that every time we took the field, we expected to win. As defending state champions, we knew there would be a target on our back all season long, and that we had to be at our best and expect everyone's best shot at knocking us off. We weren't content with living in the past year's success, but building on it and reaching the pinnacle again. Because of this, they put in the extra film time, and spent the needed time studying their scouting reports each week so that, when we took the field, we felt like we knew our opponent's offense and defense as well as they did. They truly played the entire season with a champion's attitude.

What piece of advice would you give to a head coach who wants to win a state championship?

Success never comes easy. There has to be commitment on your end as a coach to outwork the other coaches in your league, and to constantly improve as a coach through clinics, film study, reading, and visiting with your peers. There also has to be commitment and leadership from your players. They have to want to be successful and be committed to getting up early in the summer to lift, and be willing to sacrifice parts of their personal lives for the benefit of the team. I think coaches also must encourage their kids to be athletes and not just football players, and be flexible in that you need to coach to your personnel but keep continuity in your system so that you can adjust on the fly.

What do you consider the one most important aspect of your championship team this year? How did you develop that in your program?

I think the most important aspect of our team this year was our winning attitude. I could look into the eyes of our seniors and be confident that they wouldn't let us lose. No matter how close the game was or how poorly we may have been playing early in the game. When push came to shove, I knew they would lead us with their refuse-to-lose attitude. This isn't something, as a coach, that you teach, but rather something you can preach. I had a group with heart, passion, and desire. All I needed to do was facilitate the motivation and schematics to let them go out and execute it, and in turn they would leave it all out on the field every Saturday.

New Hampshire Division 2

Coach: Travis Cote

School: Bishop Guertin High School

City: Nashua

2011 Record: 9-3, 7-1

Championship Game Results:

| Bishop Guertin | 16 |
| Dover | 7 |

State Championships at School: 7

Years as Head Coach: 8

Years at Current School: 2

State Championships Won as Head Coach: 1

Noteworthy: The 2011 Championship was Bishop Guertin High School's seventh state championship in eight years.

What did you do differently this year from the other programs in your league, your section, your state that enabled your success as a state champion?

We make sure we play all three aspects of the game: offense, defense, and special teams. Our special teams play this year was outstanding. We had three successful fake punts, a punt return for a touchdown, and a kickoff return for a touchdown. Use special teams to change momentum.

What piece of advice would you give to a head coach who wants to win a state championship?

Stay true to what you believe in. Don't think you need to run the schemes that other teams do because they have success with it. Work hard at what you do, and be good at it.

What do you consider the one most important aspect of your championship team this year? How did you develop that in your program?

Your players need to trust you and buy into the offensive and defensive schemes that you implement.

New Hampshire Division 5

Coach: Eric Cumba

School: St. Thomas Aquinas High School

City: Dover

2011 Record: 11-0, 9-0

Championship Game Results:

St. Thomas Aquinas	49
Windham	28

State Championships at School: 7

Years as Head Coach: 1

Years at Current School: 1

State Championships Won as Head Coach: 1

Noteworthy: This was his first championship, in his first year ever as a head coach.

What did you do differently this year from the other programs in your league, your section, your state that enabled your success as a state champion?

This year, in my first year as a head coach, we remade the culture of the program. We implemented a whole new system and created a tempo that the kids have never experienced before. Week after week, we stressed the importance of what we were doing and continued to challenge our young men and raise the level of expectation. As a result, we brought the program to a level that not only our kids, but our opponents had never seen, and it was evident on a week-to-week basis.

What piece of advice would you give to a head coach who wants to win a state championship?

I would tell another coach to stay the course and stay true to your philosophy and the culture you are trying to create as a coach. Challenge your players on a day-to-day basis, and hold them accountable for their mistakes. Once they buy into what you are preaching, not only will they be successful football players, but they will be successful people as well.

What do you consider the one most important aspect of your championship team this year? How did you develop that in your program?

The most important factor in our championship season is the fact that our kids bought into what we were trying to do. When you are in a new situation, change isn't always welcomed, but we were fortunate enough to be in a great situation. On a day-to-day basis, our football players were challenged to make them themselves better, and we never took a day off from stressing that philosophy. Whether it was finishing a run or a block in a team period, being a good teammate and giving a quality look during an individual rep or knowing all the answers to the questions during a film session, we raised the level of expectation and the kids met us head on.

New Hampshire Division IV

Coach: Gary Leonard
School: Trinity High School
City: Manchester
2011 Record: 11-1, 9-0

Championship Game Results:

    Trinity   30
    Plymouth   14

State Championships at School: 3

Years as Head Coach: 14

Years at Current School: 5

State Championships Won as Head Coach: 2

What did you do differently this year from the other programs in your league, your section, your state that enabled your success as a state champion?

What piece of advice would you give to a head coach who wants to win a state championship?

What do you consider the one most important aspect of your championship team this year? How did you develop that in your program?

I have been a football coach for 32 years. I coached the same way; right or wrong, that is what I believe. I win when my players are better than the other teams, and I lose when they are not. It is very simple.

    I have no wisdom more valuable than anyone else. If my X's are better than your O's, I win; if not, I lose.

New Jersey Division North 2 I

Coach: Ed Sadloch

School: Cedar Grove High School

City: Cedar Grove

2011 Record: 10-2, 5-0

Championship Game Results:

    Cedar Grove   34
    Weequahic (Newark)   21

State Championships at School: 7

Years as Head Coach: 34

Years at Current School: 22

State Championships Won as Head Coach: 5

What did you do differently this year from the other programs in your league, your section, your state that enabled your success as a state champion?

I don't think (nor do I want to speak) about what other coaches do or do not do in their programs. At Cedar Grove, we have a philosophy about everything: offense, defense, special teams, practice organization, staff meetings, off-season for players and coaches. These philosophies do not really change over the years. They might be adjusted if we find a better way of doing things, but for the most part they are the foundation of our program. Hopefully, our team gets better each day, and by the time we get to the state playoffs, we are hitting on all cylinders. This season, we started off real strong, winning six straight games and then lost two games in a row before we won our last four. Injuries played a factor in those losses, as did the fact that both teams we lost to were playoff teams in a larger group. I would like to believe, at Cedar Grove, we coach our players up and stay consistent with the philosophy we have developed over the years.

What piece of advice would you give to a head coach who wants to win a state championship?

It took me 20 years to win a state championship. Our teams got close a few times, but we could never get it done. Looking back now, I think both the staff and I were too conservative in our approach to playoff games. I think we played not to lose instead of going out trying to win. After we won our first in 2000, we became a little more wide open and developed an attitude that "You have to beat us," not "What do we have to do to beat our opponent?" Since we took that approach. we have been in the finals six times winning five (with our most recent in 2011). If you want to win a state championship, you must be willing to take risks in all phases of the game. Also, your players have to believe they can win, and that will come from you and your coaches. If everyone is on the same page, you have a good chance to succeed.

What do you consider the one most important aspect of your championship team this year? How did you develop that in your program?

In 2010, we had our second losing season in 20 years. That season snapped an 18-year winning streak and a 13-year playoff run. This was due to a couple of things. We graduated 18 seniors, and we were forced to play a number of underclassmen who had little or no varsity playing experience. We really didn't have the senior leadership because of this lack of playing experience. Every team we played against were primarily senior-dominated teams. With that being said, we went 4-6 and lost two games by one point. If things went our way, we could have been 6-4. After that season, we decided we needed everyone on the same page and everyone had to work together. We had a mantra of "We, not me." It started in off-season conditioning. Players who worked hard received a wristband with "We, not me" on it. Pretty soon, more and more players bought in and wanted to wear that wristband. Our players got the winning attitude back, and the rest is history.

I firmly believe that people, not schemes, win championships. Our 2011 season proved that. We were primarily an underclassmen football team and look forward to 2012.

New Jersey South 1

Coach: Greg Maccarone

School: Glassboro High School

City: Glassboro

2011 Record: 10-2, 3-1

Championship Game Results:

| Glassboro | 41 |
| Pennsville Memorial | 13 |

State Championships at School: 5

Years as Head Coach: No response

Years at Current School: No response

State Championships Won as Head Coach: No response

What did you do differently this year from the other programs in your league, your section, your state that enabled your success as a state champion?

We lift and practice during the off-season. We have excellent talent, and as a staff we put in hours watching film and preparing for our opponents.

What piece of advice would you give to a head coach who wants to win a state championship?

It is a long process that takes a minimum of four years to accomplish.

What do you consider the one most important aspect of your championship team this year? How did you develop that in your program?

Staying healthy is a major key to winning a state title. We are able to accomplish this by having light/limited hitting in practice and intense practices.

New Jersey North 2 IV

Coach: Dan Higgins

School: Piscataway High School

City: Piscataway

2011 Record: 10-2, 6-2

Championship Game Results:

    Piscataway   41
    Elizabeth   34

State Championships at School: 8

Years as Head Coach: 9

Years at Current School: 21

State Championships Won as Head Coach: 5

What did you do differently this year from the other programs in your league, your section, your state that enabled your success as a state champion?

We were able to maximize our potential weekly by utilizing a game plan and skill sets of the players to attack against the weakness of the opposing team. We would run more if they had trouble with the run game, we would tweak the defense to add more or less to the box to defend and attack what they did well, and we always used special teams to help dictate field position.

What piece of advice would you give to a head coach who wants to win a state championship?

Pay attention to your players, and focus on trying to get the most out of them. You must put the toughest players on the field and play to their strengths. Flexibility in schemes is very important; don't try to force plays/schemes on them that they can't get. Motivate them daily with goals and themes for the week. If you believe in them, they will believe in you.

What do you consider the one most important aspect of your championship team this year? How did you develop that in your program?

They were playing for each other and not themselves. It took a tremendous amount of group mentoring and teaching. We would read any newspaper articles or relative current events that spoke to the team-first mentality. After our second and final loss of the season, a player asked to show a motivational video, How Bad Do You Want It. It turned the season around. We never lost another game. We won nine straight and entered the playoffs as the last seed and played every game away, but we never forgot who we were playing for and won a second straight state championship.

New York Division A

Coach: Matt Gallagher

School: Maine-Endwell High School

City: Endwell

2011 Record: 14-0, 3-0

Championship Game Results:

| Maine-Endwell | 27 |
| Burnt Hills-Ballston Lake | 20 |

State Championships at School: 2

Years as Head Coach: 4

Years at Current School: 4

State Championships Won as Head Coach: 1

What did you do differently this year from the other programs in your league, your section, your state that enabled your success as a state champion?

It was a combination of what we have been doing along with some new things we added. We did change our offensive system to fit our players' strengths, but we feel the culture that we have established over the last four years was the base for the success. There has to be a strong foundation to allow the changes to be successful.

What piece of advice would you give to a head coach who wants to win a state championship?

Believe winning a state championship is possible. You must instill the belief in your coaches, players, and everyone involved in your program that it is attainable. A culture needs to be established that allows everyone to believe it can happen.

What do you consider the one most important aspect of your championship team this year? How do you develop that in your program?

The single-most important aspect of this year's team was its character. We stress the following from day one, every day:

- What happens off the field is equally as important as what happens on the field.
- The big things don't happen without the little things happening first.
- Doing the right things must become a habit.

And, most importantly, we stress that we are a team, not a bunch of individuals.

New York Division D

Coach: Tim McMullen

School: Letchworth High School

City: Gainesville

2011 Record: 12-1, 5-0

Championship Game Results:

    Letchworth   27

    Chester   0

State Championships at School: 1

Years as Head Coach: 11

Years at Current School: 30

State Championships Won as Head Coach: 1

What did you do differently this year from the other programs in your league, your section, your state that enabled your success as a state champion?

What piece of advice would you give to a head coach who wants to win a state championship?

What do you consider the one most important aspect of your championship team this year? How did you develop that in your program?

This year in particular, we did not change anything. This year's state title comes from years of commitment in the off-season, focusing on goals set years before. A core of players (along with the staff) buying into a belief system and consistently committing their time to the weight room and each other. This commitment and belief led to higher performance levels on the field, and more importantly, a confidence and togetherness that was unmatched throughout the season. By the time the state tournament came around, there were no egos on the field. Our sole intention was to work as hard as we could (collectively) on every down (just as we had done for years in the weight room on every rep).

As a coach, I believe we must get in the bubble of each player. They must know you care about them as individuals off the field even more than on the field. Once they feel that true caring from you, and that is combined with the passion and commitment in the weight room, they will go to the wall for you and the staff. When your leaders or captains feel this way, it becomes pervasive, and it will lift the whole program.

North Carolina 3AA

Coach: John Roscoe

School: Northern Guilford High School

City: Greensboro

2011 Record: 14-1, 7-0

Championship Game Results:

    Providence Day   31
    Crest (Shelby)   7

State Championships at School: 2

Years as Head Coach: 34

Years at Current School: 5

State Championships Won as Head Coach: 3

Noteworthy: The 2011 Championship was Northern Guilford High School's second state championship in three years.

What did you do differently this year from the other programs in your league, your section, your state that enabled your success as a state champion?

What piece of advice would you give to a head coach who wants to win a state championship?

What do you consider the one most important aspect of your championship team this year? How did you develop that in your program?

As coaches, we tried to keep it as closely to 2010 as possible because we wanted to repeat as champions in 2011. AIR was our catch phase this year, meaning "All in repeat." We continued to work on fundamentals each practice even before the state championship game. Each playoff game, we stressed some aspect of teamwork and brotherhood.

North Carolina NCISAA 1

Coach: Bruce Hardin

School: Providence Day High School

City: Charlotte

2011 Record: 11-2, 2-1

Championship Game Results:

    Providence Day   20
    Charlotte Country Day   14

State Championships at School: 1

Years as Head Coach: 47

Years at Current School: 4

State Championships Won as Head Coach: 3

What did you do differently this year from the other programs in your league, your section, your state that enabled your success as a state champion?

What piece of advice would you give to a head coach who wants to win a state championship?

What do you consider the one most important aspect of your championship team this year? How did you develop that in your program?

The chemistry that players created among themselves was influenced by our senior leaders. There were no egos to feed, and the players truly believed in each other being accountable for doing their assignments well. The coaches taught on the field each day and kept practices well-organized. Watching film and making the daily improvements was a big help in the stretch run of the playoffs. Our quarterback managed the games well, and the defense was productive in getting the ball to our offense with good field position. Blocking punts, field goals, returning punts, and kickoffs were a big part of our game plan and were executed by the players. The support from the community was inspiring to all of us. This season was a "memory forever." We did not discuss or talk about championships, just "win the day."

North Carolina 2A

Coach: Jeff Craddock

School: Tarboro High School

City: Tarboro

2011 Record: 13-2, 5-1

Championship Game Results:

    Tarboro   39
    Lincolnton 36

State Championships at School: 4

Years as Head Coach: 8

Years at Current School: 8

State Championships Won as Head Coach: 3

What did you do differently this year from the other programs in your league, your section, your state that enabled your success as a state champion?

I believe we get a competitive edge during our off-season training program. We work extremely hard in our off-season, and our weight lifting/speed development program is run just like a practice. The players are pushed to extreme levels, and a total commitment to our program is required. Every class at Tarboro High wants the chance to become state champions, and they are reminded on a daily basis that only one team in the state will be the best. Never let your opponent outwork you on any given day. Our phrase is: "Somebody is going to get better today; it might as well be Tarboro."

What piece of advice would you give to a head coach who wants to win a state championship?

My main piece of advice would be: "You win with good people." Surround yourself with players and coaches who you can trust and who have the same vision as you do in regard to becoming state champions. Once you have that in place, maintain a consistent level of discipline. Players need to know the level of expectations. In the beginning, you will lose players who you think will help you win because they may be good athletes, but they do not understand what it really takes to be the best. In the long run, you will get the athlete who has a great attitude and understands expectations, and your program will be built to win for the long haul.

What do you consider the one most important aspect of your championship team this year? How did you develop that in your program?

Our football team expects to win every time they step on the field. This has been developed by years of hard work and dedication to our program. We believe we outprepare every opponent we face. We do this by our off-season and summer programs and also intense film study of our opponents through the week. One of our favorite mottos is "The will to prepare to win must be greater than the will to win." In this year's playoffs alone, we won two games by two, and two games by three. We were losing in the fourth quarter in three of the four games. We just believe we will always find a way.

North Dakota AAA

Coach: Mark Gibson

School: Bismarck High School

City: Bismarck

2011 Record: 11-1, 5-1

Championship Game Results:

Bismarck	21
Century (Bismarck)	3

State Championships at School: 11

Years as Head Coach: 13

Years at Current School: 13

State Championships Won as Head Coach: 4

What did you do differently this year from the other programs in your league, your section, your state that enabled your success as a state champion?

Most of the teams now are doing what we do, which is putting time into the weight room and attending summer team camps. A few years ago, we were one of the only teams that did this, but now everyone has tried to copy what we do in the off-season.

What piece of advice would you give to a head coach who wants to win a state championship?

Time. You have to go the extra mile at all times: winter, spring, and especially summer. I don't have much of life during the summer. I am either running young-aged camps here in town, taking our team to different team camps and spending six hours a day in the weight room. You must make the commitment if you expect your kids to.

What do you consider the one most important aspect of your championship team this year? How did you develop that in your program?

Our kids believe they are going to make it to the finals and win every season. We talk from day one about making it to the finals and anything else would be a disappointment. We have a great tradition here, which helps us a great deal because every group doesn't want to be the team to disappoint past players who built this program. We talk about that daily.

Ohio Division 6

Coach: Tim Goodwin

School: Marion Local High School

City: Maria Stein

2011 Record: 13-2, 7-1

Championship Game Results:

Marion Local	61
Buckeye Central (New Washington)	21

State Championships at School: 5

Years as Head Coach: 13

Years at Current School: 13

State Championships Won as Head Coach: 5

What did you do differently this year from the other programs in your league, your section, your state that enabled your success as a state champion?

I don't know, other than stay healthy and improve as the year went on. It is hard to say what the other teams are doing.

What piece of advice would you give to a head coach who wants to win a state championship?

Do not coach just to win a state championship. Coach for the right reasons, such as loving the game, being a part of a team, being a positive influence on young people, using the platform of football to affect the community, etc. I have won five state championships, and I can tell you that it can feel very empty if that is all that you are coaching for.

What do you consider the one most important aspect of your championship team this year? How did you develop that in your program?

Being flexible and able to adapt to changing situations. We focus on fundamentals and conditioning. If you have those, you can change your schemes without being too complex of confusing. Having a vision, what do you want your team to look like? You need to constantly work your program and vision.

Ohio Division IV

Coach: Joe Harbour

School: Norwayne High School

City: Creston

2011 Record: 14-1, 6-1

Championship Game Results:

Norwayne	48
Kenton	42

State Championships at School: 1

Years as Head Coach: 3

Years at Current School: 3

State Championships Won as Head Coach: 1

What did you do differently this year from the other programs in your league, your section, your state that enabled your success as a state champion?

First off, we had an exceptional group of kids with a senior class of strong leaders who have been talking about, believing in, and building toward the goal of a state championship since they were seventh graders. This past off-season, we challenged them to make that dream a reality by dedicating, working, and pushing themselves at a level they never have before with the help of an outside trainer and "agent of change," Rick Cugini. This intense off-season not only prepared us physically for the 15-week run it takes to win a state title in Ohio, but more importantly it built us up mentally and developed our character (or, as we called it, "heart power") to a point that no opponent, circumstance, or challenge ever seemed too hard or caused us to doubt ourselves.

What piece of advice would you give to a head coach who wants to win a state championship?

It is just as important to develop players' mental toughness and "heart power" as it is to develop their physical talents and skills. In crucial moments, these often are more important in the determination of success and failure than physical attributes.

Also, do not be afraid of letting kids sit and talk about lofty goals, as long as you reinforce that such goals can only be achieved through dedication, hard work, and taking things one workout, one practice, and one game at a time.

What do you consider the one most important aspect of your championship team this year? How did you develop that in your program?

Dedication to the team goal or mission and complete true belief that it can indeed be reached. Intense off-season training and character building reinforced our sense of commitment as well as helped us develop a "no doubts" mentality that as long as we fight together as a team, there are no limits to what we can do. This was displayed no more clearly than in the state finals game when we fell behind for the very first time in the game late in the fourth quarter in a manner that could have broken the spirit of many teams. Our senior quarterback walked into the huddle simply said, "No doubts, we got this," and then we marched down the field to score the game-winning touchdown with 30 seconds left in the game.

Ohio Division 2

Coach: Maurice Douglass
School: Trotwood-Madison High School
City: Trotwood
2011 Record: 15-0, 4-0

Championship Game Results:

| Trotwood-Madison | 42 |
| Avon | 28 |

State Championships at School: 1

Years as Head Coach: 11

Years at Current School: 11

State Championships Won as Head Coach: 1

What did you do differently this year from the other programs in your league, your section, your state that enabled your success as a state champion?

We made it a point of emphasis to finish the deal this season, after losing in the state championship game last season.

What piece of advice would you give to a head coach who wants to win a state championship?

The biggest advice that I could give another coach is make connections with the kids. Take it one play at a time each week. Focus on not giving up impact plays.

What do you consider the one most important aspect of your championship team this year? How did you develop that in your program?

Our team chemistry was great. The players had a great drive to finish the deal this season. We worked on being selfless and being team first mentality. Our motto was: "If we win, you win."

Oklahoma 6A

Coach: Kirk Fridrich

School: Union High School

City: Tulsa

2011 Record: 14-1, 6-1

Championship Game Results:

| Union High School | 23 |
| Broken Arrow | 2 |

State Championships at School: 8

Years as Head Coach: 10

Years at Current School: 5

State Championships Won as Head Coach: 4

What did you do differently this year from the other programs in your league, your section, your state that enabled your success as a state champion?

I'm not sure because I don't know what the other schools are doing. But I do know what I believe makes a difference in our program.

What piece of advice would you give to a head coach who wants to win a state championship?

We believe that you develop the whole athlete with the mind-set of becoming a champion in every area of life. We ask our players to live like a champion.

What do you consider the one most important aspect of your championship team this year? How did you develop that in your program?

We believe that you become a champion first, and then you win championships. Winning a championship doesn't make you a champion in our eyes. Doing things right all the time will make it habit-forming. It is easy to do it right on game night if you are in the habit of doing it all the time: practice effort, academics, citizenship, character, community service, etc.

Oregon 2A

Coach: Kevin Swift

School: Gold Beach High School

City: Gold Beach

2011 Record: 13-0, 5-0

Championship Game Results:

Gold Beach	30
Scio	0

State Championships at School: 3

Years as Head Coach: 15

Years at Current School: 15

State Championships Won as Head Coach: 2

Noteworthy: In the 2011 season, Gold Beach High School was the Sunset League Hybrid Champion.

What did you do differently this year from the other programs in your league, your section, your state that enabled your success as a state champion?

Gold Beach High School has played in five state title games in the last seven years, winning two and losing three. Our kids and community are committed to our working all of our opponents in league and in the state. Investing more, therefore, we play more determined to win, rather than hoping to win. Also, we returned to a true option quarterback, rather than a great quarterback, but not necessarily an option quarterback.

What piece of advice would you give to a head coach who wants to win a state championship?

Be true to your beliefs. Remember, kids are not just listening to you, but watching you. This generation is very visual in their learning; therefore, you had better be working hard visibly if you want your team to work hard. My kids and community work 24/7 on our program because I do, and they can see it, so they do, too.

What do you consider the one most important aspect of your championship team this year? How did you develop that in your program?

Team chemistry is everything. The 2010 state runner-up had more talent than this year's 2011 championship team did, but they could not all get along. We stressed respect and had several team-building activities.

Pennsylvania Division AAAA

Coach: Glen McNamee

School: Central Dauphin High School

City: Harrisburg

2011 Record: 15-1, 6-0

Championship Game Results:

| Central Dauphin | 14 |
| North Penn (Lansdale) | 7 |

State Championships at School: 1

Years as Head Coach: 6

Years at Current School: 6

State Championships Won as Head Coach: 1

What did you do differently this year from the other programs in your league, your section, your state that enabled your success as a state champion?

I believe the most important thing that separated us from other teams this year was the willingness of our players to buy into the core philosophy of our football program. We also had an extremely experienced, knowledgeable, and talented coaching staff that did a great job of instilling our core philosophy. In the good times and in the times of adversity, everyone in the program stuck to that philosophy and kept the train on the tracks.

What piece of advice would you give to a head coach who wants to win a state championship?

My advice would be that championships should be viewed as a by-product more than a goal. The goals should be other specific and measureable things that lead to the creation of a positive experience for the players.

What do you consider the one most important aspect of your championship team this year? How did you develop that in your program?

One of the most important ingredients in our program is the emphasis on selflessness. Selflessness is one of our core values, and we look to highlight it every chance we can as a coaching staff. Through the course of a high school football season, so many moments of adversity can derail a team. Selflessness, and the togetherness that comes from true selflessness, can carry a team through those moments.

Rhode Island Division 1

Coach: Keith Croft

School: Bishop Hendricken High School

City: Warwick

2011 Record: 9-2, 6-2

Championship Game Results:

| Bishop Hendricken | 17 |
| La Salle Academy (Providence) | 14 |

State Championships at School: 7

Years as Head Coach: 6

Years at Current School: 6

State Championships Won as Head Coach: 2

What did you do differently this year from the other programs in your league, your section, your state that enabled your success as a state champion?

One of the unique things that we do at Bishop Hendricken is an off-season point program, where athletes earn points not only for weight lifting, but also for good grades, community service, and playing other sports. This allows us to not only monitor our students during the off-season, but also encourages them to actively engage in the school community.

What piece of advice would you give to a head coach who wants to win a state championship?

I would prepare the same whether your goal is a state championship or to finish with a .500 record. It is the preparation and consistency within your program that will cultivate the championship success.

What do you consider the one most important aspect of your championship team this year? How did you develop that in your program?

The most important part of our team this year was their work ethic, specifically with the strength and conditioning. It was developed as a program from the winter, into the summer, and through the season. It helped to keep us healthy and focused.

South Carolina Class 4A Division 1

Coach: Chris Miller

School: Byrnes High School

City: Duncan

2011 Record: 13-2, 6-0

Championship Game Results:

| Byrnes | 31 |
| Gaffney | 24 |

State Championships at School: 11

Years as Head Coach: 16

Years at Current School: 5

State Championships Won as Head Coach: 4

What did you do differently this year from the other programs in your league, your section, your state that enabled your success as a state champion?

Never did anything differently as far as our program goes. Concentrated on things throughout the year where we thought needed some help. Our kids believe and continue to work hard and listen to our adjustments.

What piece of advice would you give to a head coach who wants to win a state championship?

Find out what others are doing that are winning in your area, see if you can use some of that in your program and continue to build. Continue to learn from others. Getting the kids to buy into your system.

What do you consider the one most important aspect of your championship team this year? How did you develop that in your program?

Confidence and believing we could win. Something that has been produced through the years that the seniors continue to carry to the next team.

South Carolina SCISA – A

Coach: Neil Minton

School: Colleton Prep Academy

City: Walterboro

2011 Record: 9-2, 3-0

Championship Game Results:

| Colleton Prep | 29 |
| Holly Hill Academy | 8 |

State Championships at School: No response

Years as Head Coach: No response

Years at Current School: No Response

State Championships Won as Head Coach: No response

What did you do differently this year from the other programs in your league, your section, your state that enabled your success as a state champion?

What piece of advice would you give to a head coach who wants to win a state championship?

What do you consider the one most important aspect of your championship team this year? How did you develop that in your program?

The key for us was a great attitude and leadership from our seniors. They led us in the off-season and made our weight program a significant role in our success.

Having a staff that genuinely cares for the kids and the program is also essential. Basically, we (as coaches) and our players bought into our system and really worked hard on fundamentals and being mentally and physically prepared. The kids had a goal, committed to it, and obtained it.

South Carolina Class 4A Division II

Coach: Chuck Reedy

School: Goose Creek High School

City: Goose Creek

2011 Record: 14-1, 4-0

Championship Game Results:

| Goose Creek | 37 |
| Greenwood | 21 |

State Championships at School: 1

Years as Head Coach: 18

Years at Current School: 10

State Championships Won as Head Coach: 1

Noteworthy: Coach Chuck Reedy also won a national championship with Clemson University in 1981.

What did you do differently this year from the other programs in your league, your section, your state that enabled your success as a state champion?

What piece of advice would you give to a head coach who wants to win a state championship?

What do you consider the one most important aspect of your championship team this year? How did you develop that in your program?

The year before I took the job, the team was 0-11. We were so bad that our goal was just to improve every day. Over the years, we have never deviated from that and preach that if every player will get a little better every day—whether it be during practice or off-season, get a little better today—multiply that by 75 players, and we have made progress as a team. Using this approach, we have improved every year, culminating with a 27-2 record the last two years and the state championship this season.

As for the questions: 1) We stress being tough, physical, and hard-nosed, and playing with great effort for 48 minutes. 2) Have a plan and philosophy, and stick with it. Do not deviate. 3) We are a run-oriented offense (rushed for 364 yards per game, 48 points per game). We practice and preach being physical on offense, defense, and the kicking game.

South Carolina SCISA Division AAA

Coach: Erik Kimrey

School: Hammond School

City: Columbia

2011 Record: 12-1, 8-1

Championship Game Results:

Hammond	13
Wilson Hall (Sumter)	9

State Championships at School: 12

Years as Head Coach: 8

Years at Current School: 8

State Championships Won as Head Coach: 6

What did you do differently this year from the other programs in your league, your section, your state that enabled your success as a state champion?

It would be very difficult for me to speak of that intelligently due to my lack of comprehensive knowledge of the inner workings of other programs in our league.

What piece of advice would you give to a head coach who wants to win a state championship?

Let your authority be based on authenticity, not rhetoric, personality, or vain speech. Your ultimate pursuit is one of a mentor and teacher. It is certainly not wins.

What do you consider the one most important aspect of your championship team this year? How did you develop that in your program?

I hope that it is striving in gratitude. It's far from perfect, but it is our continual goal. It must start from an appreciation for the life and talents that we have been given and from this point, derives a deep-seated desire to honor these talents each and every moment of every rep of every practice of every week of every game of every season of our entire careers of our entire lives.

South Carolina SCISA-AA

Coach: Tommy Lewis

School: Hilton Head Christian Academy

City: Hilton Head Island

2011 Record: 13-0, 5-0

Championship Game Results:

Hilton Head Christian Academy	35
Thomas Sumter Academy	21

State Championships at School: 3

Years as Head Coach: 12

Years at Current School: 9

State Championships Won as Head Coach: 3

What did you do differently this year from the other programs in your league, your section, your state that enabled your success as a state champion?

What piece of advice would you give to a head coach who wants to win a state championship?

What do you consider the one most important aspect of your championship team this year? How did you develop that in your program?

While we obviously coach the fundamentals, day in and day out, our staff works diligently on developing the whole person with our players. Our philosophy is Christ-centered and challenges the young men we coach spiritually, socially, academically, and athletically. We teach and model servant-leadership and work hard to foster team chemistry and unity. And just like any great team across America, you've got to have great kids and families and great school support. We've been blessed with both over the years.

South Carolina Class AAA

Coach: Strait Herron

School: South Pointe High School

City: Rock Hill

2011 Record: 14-1, 5-0

Championship Game Results:

South Point	42
Bluffton	27

State Championships at School: 2

Years as Head Coach: 1

Years at Current School: 1

State Championships Won as Head Coach: 1

What did you do differently this year from the other programs in your league, your section, your state that enabled your success as a state champion?

First off, you need to know that I am a first-year head coach. I was coaching at South Pointe as the defensive coordinator until I was promoted. I don't like to make a comparison of the changes that I have made because of the sensitivity of the issue with the head coach who was here before. I hope you understand. I will tell you about what we do and what I believe is important.

I don't know if we do anything differently than others, but we have assured our players that we truly, genuinely care about all of them. Each of them knows—whether he is a superstar, starter, or practice player—that we are going to treat them equally. What one gets, they all get. My favorite quote, which I tell our coaching staff that we will live by, is: "They don't care how much you know until they know how much you care."

What piece of advice would you give to a head coach who wants to win a state championship?

The best piece of advice I think I can give is to create a program that attracts athletes. You can't "win it all" without athletes. You are not going to have athletes if you do not run a program that players want to be a part of. To create that program, it must have structure. Players want to be led. They don't want to be harassed (being too strict) but definitely not given free rein to do as they please. Players want structure. Give them the expectations, and then hold them to those expectations.

What do you consider the one most important aspect of your championship team this year? How did you develop that in your program?

I think the most important part was attitude. South Pointe has been successful in football since the school opened only seven short years ago. Our players know that we have gained that success because of their basic God-given athletic ability. This year, I challenged our players by asking them "How good could you be?" The players knew they had to change their attitude to reach their best potential. That change in attitude created a better work ethic, more team unity, more dedication, and more individual character, which I believe is imperative to winning.

South Carolina Class AA Division 1

Coach: Art Craig

School: Timberland High School

City: St. Stephen

2011 Record: 14-1, 4-1

Championship Game Results:

Timberland	20
Woodruff	3

State Championships at School: 1

Years as Head Coach: 14

Years at Current School: 11

State Championships Won as Head Coach: 1

What did you do differently this year from the other programs in your league, your section, your state that enabled your success as a state champion?

On offense, we implemented the pistol to our flex bone, and it gave us the ability to spread the field and allowed our quarterback (5'6" / 160 lbs) a chance to make the plays in the crunch when we had to. We allowed our players the ability to make the plays when they had to. We were not that far off from winning the state the past few years (51-4 the past four years). We decided as a team that to beat us, you would have to beat the whole team, and the one game we lost this year brought us closer together. We didn't blame players or coaches; we all took responsibility.

What piece of advice would you give to a head coach who wants to win a state championship?

Don't be afraid to coach outside the box. This year in the quarterfinals, semi, and finals, I convinced the players that if you get me there, then I will call any play necessary to win. If we lose, then let it be because the other team was better, not because we didn't give our kids a chance to make plays.

What do you consider the one most important aspect of your championship team this year? How did you develop that in your program?

This wasn't the most talented team that I have had, but it was the best team. These kids liked each other and respected each other and their views. We pushed each other, enjoyed each other, and people were not afraid to laugh or cry with this group.

South Dakota Class 9AA

Coach: Jeff VanLeur

School: Bridgewater/Emery/Ethan

Cities: Bridgewater, Emery, and Ethan

2011 Record: 11-1, 4-1

Championship Game Results:

    Bridgewater/Emery/Ethan 36
    Kimball/White Lake   24

State Championships at School: 5

Years as Head Coach: 32

Years at Current School: 32

State Championships Won as Head Coach: 5

What did you do differently this year from the other programs in your league, your section, your state that enabled your success as a state champion?

What did we do differently from other programs around our state? That's a tough question because I'm not sure what other programs do, but I will give you a few things that I believe has made our program successful throughout the years.

- Coaching staff: We have a great staff, who have all brought into our system. A couple our past players know what I want taught and how I want it taught.
- Continuity: We run the same offense year after year and all through our 7th through 12th grades. I believe by the time our players become varsity players, they know our system well.
- Acceleration program: We run an acceleration program during the summer months, in which we have a high percentage of our players participate. Last year, we had 97 percent of our players attend.

What piece of advice would you give to a head coach who wants to win a state championship?

Teach players how to work. I think kids today need to be taught how to work hard. It seems to be a lost characteristic that kids do not learn. Also gaining trust for your program. Getting players to trust in the coaching staff, their teammates, and themselves.

What do you consider the one most important aspect of your championship team this year? How did you develop that in your program?

This year, our most significant aspect was: believe. Our players believed we were going to be successful this year. Their work ethic was second to none in-season and out of season. We were unselfish in the fact that we had no "I" players, which meant we played as a team the entire season. And lastly was trusting in each other, themselves, and the coaches. You could see that trust in our players' eyes after every play. Each of them knew that they were going to give whatever it took to get the job done along with knowing that the guy next to them was going to do the same thing.

South Dakota 9A

Coach: Lenny Schroeder

School: Canistota High School

City: Canistota

2011 Record: 12-0, 5-0

Championship Game Results:

    Canistota   66
    Wall   6

State Championships at School: 2

Years as Head Coach: 21

Years at Current School: 7

State Championships Won as Head Coach: 2

What did you do differently this year from the other programs in your league, your section, your state that enabled your success as a state champion?

We try to run an offense and defense that is unique to the Canistota Hawks. Running a unique offense and defense makes other teams have to prepare for us instead of defending just another I formation team or 4-3 defense. We run an option-based offense, where our players all have specific roles to play. Each player has to perform as if he has the ball or the play is coming to him. Defensively, each player has a lane to fill.

What piece of advice would you give to a head coach who wants to win a state championship?

Coach what you know. Don't go with the latest fad and be disappointed when you don't know how to coach it. If you need help, go get it.

What do you consider the one most important aspect of your championship team this year? How did you develop that in your program?

Weight lifting is the major component to our success. In our conference, if you are not strong enough, you will get pounded. We play in the toughest nine-man conference in the state of South Dakota. We developed the importance of lifting by making it the sole criteria for if a player letters or not. Quarters of play have nothing to do with whether a player letters or not. Who is to say that a freshman hasn't worked as hard as a senior, just because the senior plays more? Our players have to lift 90 percent of the scheduled lifting days during the season. We lift two days a week during the season. Once they are hooked, getting them into the weight room during the summer is easy.

South Dakota Class 11AA

Coach: Kim Nelson

School: Roosevelt High School

City: Sioux Falls

2011 Record: 11-1, 5-1

Championship Game Results:

Roosevelt	31
Washington (Sioux Falls)	17

State Championships at School: 3

Years as Head Coach: 33

Years at Current School: 3

State Championships Won as Head Coach: 1

What did you do differently this year from the other programs in your league, your section, your state that enabled your success as a state champion?

Buy-in was our biggest difference. Our players bought into our system and believed in what we were doing in all aspects of our program.

We didn't play anyone who was not willing to do what we asked and play where we asked them to. We didn't give up on them, but playing time was the reward that seemed to motivate best.

What piece of advice would you give to a head coach who wants to win a state championship?

Believing in something bigger than you was a theme that was also effective. Our team slogan is "Team, Pride, Trust," and we were able to use that to keep us focused on our own goals.

What do you consider the one most important aspect of your championship team this year? How did you develop that in your program?

I agree that concentrating on just the things that we can control, (attitude, effort, and teamwork) kept us from wavering. We also had a ceremony to put an end to the regular season and restart the playoff season. (We burned copies of our stats and newspaper articles of regular season games.) A symbol of how the regular doesn't matter anymore—each game must be the only focus we have at playoff time.

South Dakota Class 9B

Coach: Billy Kirch

School: Waverly/South Shore School

City: Waverly

2011 Record: 12-0, 8-0

Championship Game Results:

| Waverly/South Shore | 58 |
| Avon | 24 |

State Championships at School: 1

Years as Head Coach: 1

Years at Current School: 4

State Championships Won as Head Coach: 1

What did you do differently this year from the other programs in your league, your section, your state that enabled your success as a state champion?

Kids made a year-round commitment to football.

What piece of advice would you give to a head coach who wants to win a state championship?

It all starts with trust. Coaches trust each other, coaches trust players, and most importantly, players must trust themselves, their teammates, and their coaches.

What do you consider the one most important aspect of your championship team this year? How did you develop that in your program?

Burning desire to be the best. Compete your tail off in everything you do

Tennessee Division 2 Class A

Coach: Brent Hill

School: St. George's Independent School

City: Collierville

2011 Record: 11-3, 4-1

Championship Game Results:

St. George's	28
University School of Jackson	23

State Championships at School: 2

Years as Head Coach: 1

Years at Current School: 6

State Championships Won as Head Coach: 1

What did you do differently this year from the other programs in your league, your section, your state that enabled your success as a state champion?

What piece of advice would you give to a head coach who wants to win a state championship?

What do you consider the one most important aspect of your championship team this year? How did you develop that in your program?

We at St. George's tried to focus on each week. Externally to the team and internally as a staff, we made sure that our week-to-week approach fit our seasonal goal. Our core values for the season were discussed instead of winning. The core values were: truth, respect, loyalty, commitment, and desire. Each day, we talked about our core values, and each Thursday after our walk-through practice, we had a different coach talk about a different topic that was related to our core values. Other than that, we focused on winning daily against ourselves rather than beating our opponent.

Texas 3A Division1

Coach: Thomas Sitton

School: Chapel Hill High School

City: Tyler

2011 Record: 15-0, 4-0

Championship Game Results:

Chapel Hill	20
Alvarado	19

State Championships at School: 2

Years as Head Coach: 3

Years at Current School: 3

State Championships Won as Head Coach: 1

What did you do differently this year from the other programs in your league, your section, your state that enabled your success as a state champion?

Others do it, but we feel like we have one of the best off-season and boot camps around. We teach our kids to push past their comfort zone and think about their teammates more than they do themselves.

What piece of advice would you give to a head coach who wants to win a state championship?

You have to convince your kids that the only way to be successful in life and in football is hard work. You have to convince them that we are going to be the hardest working team in the state. You have to convince them that, on Friday nights, they have to be willing to play harder, faster, and more physical than the opposing team.

What do you consider the one most important aspect of your championship team this year? How did you develop that in your program?

The most important aspects we thought helped us win this year was our ability to play with great effort, being totally unselfish football players, being able to handle adversity, and thinking about the game of football 365 days a year. We were able to teach this during off-season, leadership training, and working during football season constantly preaching to them about playing fast and physical with unbelievable effort.

Texas 5A Division 2

Coach: Willie Amendola

School: Dekaney High School

City: Houston

2011 Record: 14-2, 5-2

Championship Game Results:

Dekaney	34
Steele (Cibolo)	14

State Championships at School: 1

Years as Head Coach: 7

Years at Current School: 6

State Championships Won as Head Coach: 1

What did you do differently this year from the other programs in your league, your section, your state that enabled your success as a state champion?

It's not that we did something different this year as opposed to other years; it was more about the fact that it takes years to establish a program. We invest more time than other programs in the mental and spiritual components of football.

What piece of advice would you give to a head coach who wants to win a state championship?

Recognize the specific needs of your athletes, and develop a plan to address those needs and practice planned abandonment.

What do you consider the one most important aspect of your championship team this year? How did you develop that in your program?

Team unity and love for each other. Plan for it; practice it daily. It is the single-most influential factor. We preach common purpose, mutual dependence, and shared honor.

Texas 4A Division 1

Coach: Hank Carter

School: Lake Travis High School

City: Austin

2011 Record: 16-0, 6-0

Championship Game Results:

Lake Travis	48
Midway (Waco)	42

State Championships at School: 5

Years as Head Coach: 2

Years at Current School: 2

State Championships Won as Head Coach: 2

What did you do differently this year from the other programs in your league, your section, your state that enabled your success as a state champion?

I'm not sure what we do differently. I just know that we try to stay at the cutting edge of offensive, defensive, and strength and conditioning knowledge each year to make sure we put our kids in the best possible positions in order to succeed. I think our visits to colleges in the spring have been a tremendous help.

What piece of advice would you give to a head coach who wants to win a state championship?

My advice would be to surround yourself with the best possible staff you can find. That is a huge part of our success.

What do you consider the one most important aspect of your championship team this year? How did you develop that in your program?

I think our kids are very poised and show a lot of mental toughness. We focus on that in everything we do throughout the year.

Texas TCAF Division 1

Coach: Leroy Willis

School: Lucas Christian Academy

City: Lucas

2011 Record: 12-1, 5-0

Championship Game Results:

Lucas Christian Academy	73
Trinity (Midland)	69

State Championships at School: 1

Years as Head Coach: 9

Years at Current School: 9

State Championships Won as Head Coach: 1

What did you do differently this year from the other programs in your league, your section, your state that enabled your success as a state champion?

What piece of advice would you give to a head coach who wants to win a state championship?

What do you consider the one most important aspect of your championship team this year? How did you develop that in your program?

I can only reply to the third question because I did nothing differently than the other coaches in our league. I was fortunate enough to have better players than they did. I don't think I have advice for another coach trying to win a championship unless that advice is contained in my answer to question three.

I believe focusing on character above everything else enabled us to win a state championship. The character of the players outweighs everything else because character enables you to overcome every obstacle, confront every problem, and work together as a team without any personal agenda. In our championship game, we were beaten more than once during the game, but the character of the players would not let them give up or give less than 100 percent of themselves. Character is the ingredient champions are made of, not wins and losses.

Texas 2A Division 1

Coach: Seth Stinton

School: Melissa High School

City: Melissa

2011 Record: 13-1, 5-0

Championship Game Results:

| Melissa | 28 |
| Hempstead | 15 |

State Championships at School: 1

Years as Head Coach: 3

Years at Current School: 3

State Championships Won as Head Coach: 1

What did you do differently this year from the other programs in your league, your section, your state that enabled your success as a state champion?

We spent a great deal of time teaching fundamentals early in the season that helped us during our playoff run. We also spend a great deal of time teaching leadership skills that help to build great leaders with great character. Our senior class has great leaders.

What piece of advice would you give to a head coach who wants to win a state championship?

Work hard on the little things, and be positive throughout the entire season.

What do you consider the one most important aspect of your championship team this year? How did you develop that in your program?

We were always able to respond to adversity; no matter what happened, our kids responded like champions. I believe that our coaching staff taught our players how to respond to pressure and how to respond to those situations. We always talk about handling what we can control and doing that in a positive manner.

Texas TAPPS Division 2

Coach: Greg McClendon

School: Midland Christian School

City: Midland

2011 Record: 12-2, 5-0

Championship Game Results:

Midland Christian	35
Concordia Lutheran (Tomball)	23

State Championships at School: 10

Years as Head Coach: 14

Years at Current School: 14

State Championships Won as Head Coach: 5

What did you do differently this year from the other programs in your league, your section, your state that enabled your success as a state champion?

We were balanced on offense. We could beat you running the ball or throwing the ball. We could take what you gave us and beat you with it.

Defensively, our team was well-coached, and they played like an 11-piece machine, team-wise. We went off during the first week of two-a-days and had camp at Wayland Baptist. We became a family, as in everyone valued the team above themselves. We became family, as coaches the players allowed us to enjoy them, they followed our lead, and then they led the same direction. It was special. It went far beyond the players; the parents were just at bought in as anyone.

What piece of advice would you give to a head coach who wants to win a state championship?

If your goal is to win a state championship, change your goal. If your passions are to build young men of character, faith, and a strong work ethic, build men who will be great fathers, husbands, and sons. Build relationships that change lives. The state championships become the outcome of building what really matters.

What do you consider the one most important aspect of your championship team this year? How did you develop that in your program?

Putting first things first. Placing Christ as the most important thing in your program. The closeness of the players and coaches. The seniors had a lot to do with that; they made it about the whole team. There was no selfishness on this team. Maybe the biggest reason was, at Midland Christian, we have won five state championships since 2000, but we were four years from our last one. The drought was hard, and it helped this group to develop an attitude of "Whatever you say, coach, we will do. You have four rings; we have none. No questions asked. We will do whatever you say."

Texas TAPPS Division 1

Coach: Joe Prud'homme

School: Nolan Catholic High School

City: Fort Worth

2011 Record: 13-1, 5-1

Championship Game Results:

    Nolan Catholic   27
    Kelly Catholic (Beaumont) 10

State Championships at School: 5

Years as Head Coach: 22

Years at Current School: 19

State Championships Won as Head Coach: 5

What did you do differently this year from the other programs in your league, your section, your state that enabled your success as a state champion?

We have won five state championships since 2004 and made seven appearances. The main key has been a consistent coaching staff, excellent strength program, and tradition. We have created an offensive system that has the ability to drive the football consistently in league play and is not dependent on the big play. We are capable of the big play, but we were able to win games without it. Defensively, we were able to limit the big-play production of our opponents and force them to grind out drives, which very few were capable of doing on a consistent basis. Special teams–wise, we do focus on creating the big play; we had nine touchdowns on special teams this past year.

What piece of advice would you give to a head coach who wants to win a state championship?

Build a cohesive, competent coaching staff that is on the same page and puts the program first. Your team must master the fundamentals and be able to execute the most minor details, such as a PAT, play-action fakes, routine catches, routine tackles, run fits, etc. Build your program from the ground up with the youngest group, so that they hear the same things for four years and are able to execute your base schemes in all three phases. Playoff practices should be shorter, more focused, and have a higher intensity. This will make your team fresher, more focused, and excited for the playoff games and not leave too much on the practice field.

What do you consider the one most important aspect of your championship team this year? How did you develop that in your program?

Resiliency and attention to detail. We always preach that injuries and depth are critical elements in the game of football and that it is the most true team sport. Everybody contributes in some way either on offense, defense, special teams, or scout teams, and every player must be ready when his name is called. We got down to our fourth-string tailback in the quarterfinals, and he carried the ball six times for 48 yards and helped us on the game-clinching drive. Our quarterback did a hook slide inbounds at the opponent's three-yard line with 1:28 to go that allowed us to score and run the clock out with a five-point lead at the time. We had covered it only during August, and he performed it in late November. We rep anybody that has a chance to play, and we preach readiness in practice. Attention to detail is handled through film study and meetings. We drill our scout teams and coach them up to perform as the opponents and it was very effective for everybody involved. We study ourselves more than our opponents, and this seems to heighten our players' awareness of their performance and more honestly evaluate themselves. When you reach the point that your players can self-correct off the film and on the field, you have a great chance to be successful.

Texas 2A Division 2

Coach: Jason Herring

School: Refugio High School

City: Refugio

2011 Record: 15-0, 7-0

Championship Game Results:

Refugio	36
Cisco	35

State Championships at School: 3

Years as Head Coach: 14

Years at Current School: 5

State Championships Won as Head Coach: 2

What did you do differently this year from the other programs in your league, your section, your state that enabled your success as a state champion?

What piece of advice would you give to a head coach who wants to win a state championship?

What do you consider the one most important aspect of your championship team this year? How did you develop that in your program?

Without question, the one most important aspect of our team this year was unity. This particular team came together and held each other accountable better than any team I have ever coached. They were unified and extremely cohesive in a way that is hard to describe. "Stay linked" was our team motto; that undoubtedly was the single-most important reason we were able to win the championship.

As a coach, I try to make certain that each and every kid knows how much I love and care about him each and every day. The good Lord has blessed us 10,000 times over, and we are extremely fortunate to be in such an awesome profession.

Texas TAPPS Division IV

Coach: Pat Henke

School: Sacred Heart High School

City: Hallettsville

2011 Record: 14-1, 3-1

Championship Game Results:

Sacred Heart	21
St. Paul (Shiner)	7

State Championships at School: 12

Years as Head Coach: 31

Years at Current School: 31

State Championships Won as Head Coach: 8

What did you do differently this year from the other programs in your league, your section, your state that enabled your success as a state champion?

We did very few things differently. Good students and good athletes make good coaches. We have great administration at our school and great teachers and coaches. We did very few things differently than in our previous state championship years.

What piece of advice would you give to a head coach who wants to win a state championship?

Stick to what you believe in, but you have to be able to adjust to your kids' strengths. Do not get caught up in all the special formation stuff just because you watched it on TV and it looked good. If you have a great throwing quarterback, throw the football.

But if you have a great offensive line with good backs and your kids love to run the football, then run it. Believe me, your football players will not think running the football is boring if you are winning football games. We threw the football one time in our state championship game (a completion that led to a touchdown). My simple advice in a nutshell is that it is not so much what you know as a head coach; it is how you can adjust to what your athletes are best at doing.

What do you consider the one most important aspect of your championship team this year? How did you develop that in your program?

The most important aspect of our championship team this year was being able to run the ball, control the clock, and play great defense. Our defensive coordinator (Rick Masek) was new this year, and he did a great job. You develop this in your junior high programs. Football may have changed since I started coaching in 1976, but it still comes down to three main things if you want to be successful: blocking, tackling, and do not turn the ball over.

Texas 5A Division 1

Coach: Hal Wasson

School: Southlake Carroll Senior High School

City: Southlake

2011 Record: 16-0, 7-0

Championship Game Results:

| Carroll | 36 |
| Fort Bend Hightower (Missouri City) | 29 |

State Championships at School: 8

Years as Head Coach: 23

Years at Current School: 5

State Championships Won as Head Coach: 1

What did you do differently this year from the other programs in your league, your section, your state that enabled your success as a state champion?

We chose to really concentrate on us, physically and mentally. We identified our strengths and weaknesses in both areas. We wanted to be relentless in the pursuit of our goal and resilient in times of adversity. We spent a great deal of time on the mindset each week.

What piece of advice would you give to a head coach who wants to win a state championship?

Keep the vision alive with a great work ethic, and have the ability to persevere.

What do you consider the one most important aspect of your championship team this year? How did you develop that in your program?

We spent a great deal of time on the mind-set each week. Mental toughness—it's not the what, but the how. Mental toughness is being able to go from play to play, stay in the moment, and being able to focus. Being excellent is the ability to do common things with uncommon discipline and enthusiasm. Don't get caught up in distractions that have nothing to do with the moment/play/game, etc. This takes mental toughness, which is a learned behavior.

This takes tremendous mental and physical condition. Therefore, these are things we can control, and don't focus on the things you have no control over. Being mentality tough requires the ability to overcome adversity. You will not get there without conquering the adversity—and that's the toughest part. And this team chose to do just that. Always put the emphasis on the team.

Texas 1A Division 2

Coach: Terry Ward

School: Tenaha High School

City: Tenaha

2011 Record: 15-0, 3-0

Championship Game Results:

    Tenaha   51
    Munday   22

State Championships at School: 2

Years as Head Coach: 3

Years at Current School: 3

State Championships Won as Head Coach: 1

What did you do differently this year from the other programs in your league, your section, your state that enabled your success as a state champion?

What piece of advice would you give to a head coach who wants to win a state championship?

What do you consider the one most important aspect of your championship team this year? How did you develop that in your program?

It goes back to two things for me: relationships with the kids and trust from the kids. I asked my kids to do more things in practice this year, mentally and physically, and because of the relationship I have with them and the trust they have in me; they never hesitated, questioned, or backed down from the challenge.

Scheme-wise, we developed an offense that fit our kids and did not worry about what the trends were. Defensively, we preached tackling and turnover, which we did both every week all the way through the state game even during our bye weeks.

Texas 1A Six-Man Division 1

Coach: Michael Reed

School: Throckmorton High School

City: Throckmorton

2011 Record: 14-0, 3-0

Championship Game Results:

Throckmorton	48
Borden (Gail)	36

State Championships at School: 2

Years as Head Coach: 10

Years at Current School: 4

State Championships Won as Head Coach: 1

What did you do differently this year from the other programs in your league, your section, your state that enabled your success as a state champion?

What piece of advice would you give to a head coach who wants to win a state championship?

What do you consider the one most important aspect of your championship team this year? How did you develop that in your program?

At the conclusion of winning the state championship football game this season, I wondered, *Why this year and not the other previous three state championship trips?* It didn't take long to for me to realize that, as coaches, when the summer meetings start to take place, we always evaluate the previous season and improvements that need to be made as well as look at what game plan and house rules need to be applied in order for us to be successful for the coming season.

Following is a list of a few things that we put our focus on that we felt we didn't do as good a job with in previous seasons and wanted to add to what we were already doing. Obviously, there is much more, but I feel like when the evaluation of this state championship season came to a close, these were the things that stuck out the most as being the difference for us:

- Coach like it's your last—Put in the extra time and sacrifice. We ask our kids to do the same, but oftentimes we don't follow up with our own preaching
- Make the kids appreciate what they have—This season, we added a chore chart in the day. Example: carry water to the field, collect all the footballs prior to and after practice, sweep the locker room, etc.
- No negotiating— It never fails. If the kids say, "If we run these hard, do we have to run the next three?" it's hard to draw the line and who wins in negotiating. I think the coach and the player both lose; therefore, the team loses. So we mean what we say and say what we mean. 10 x 100s is 10 x 100s. Complete 20 passes means complete 20 passes.
- Don't let outside influences interfere with decisions—This is always difficult, especially when dealing with coffee shop drinkers, folks at the barbershop, and parents. It is critical that you deal with only issues that pertain to the athletes and could affect the team. Put the energy that might be spent justifying our decisions into the kids. The following story might clear up what I mean:

> An old man and a little boy on a donkey were on their way into town. They passed by a group of people who said, "What a shame for that old man to be walking while that perfectly able-bodied boy rides that donkey."
>
> So the boy got off the donkey, and the old man got on. They later passed by some more people who said, "Why should that little boy have to walk when they have a donkey to ride on?"
>
> So the little boy got on the donkey, and they both rode it. After a while, they passed some more people. They overheard the people say, "That poor donkey must be worn out from carrying both of them."
>
> So the little boy and old man picked up the donkey and started to carry it. They were carrying the donkey across a bridge. The weight of the donkey became just too unbearable and slipped from their grasp and went over the side of the bridge into the water and drowned.
>
> The moral of the story is: If you try to please everyone, you'll eventually lose your ass.

- Create an effective environment to learning—Having a plan for not just today, but for tomorrow, the next day, or even a month. Be flexible within that plan, but make sure that you are maximizing the time with the kids. Practice plans, meetings, etc.
- Go to church!

Utah Class 4A

Coach: Mike Favero

School: Logan High School

City: Logan

2011 Record: 14-0, 5-0

Championship Game Results:

Logan	18
East (Salt Lake City)	11

State Championships at School: 7

Years as Head Coach: 13

Years at Current School: 13

State Championships Won as Head Coach: 4

What did you do differently this year from the other programs in your league, your section, your state that enabled your success as a state champion?

Incorporated sequencing as our strength training program. Sequencing is an innovative strength training program developed by Dr. Matt Rhea, the main focus of which is training the central nervous system. We also trained metabolically by using football modeling.

What piece of advice would you give to a head coach who wants to win a state championship?

Become a passionate expert at what you believe in. Always strive to find the best way to do things and be yourself.

What do you consider the one most important aspect of your championship team this year? How did you develop that in your program?

Trust. The most important characteristic of a great leader is that he can be trusted. Trust is developed by being honest, remaining consistent, and always following through with what you say you are going to do.

Vermont Division 1

Coach: Michael Stone

School: Hartford High School

City: White River Junction

2011 Record: 11-0, 8-0

Championship Game Results:

Hartford	42
Middlebury	6

State Championships at School: 9

Years as Head Coach: 26

Years at Current School: 26

State Championships Won as Head Coach: 9

What did you do differently this year from the other programs in your league, your section, your state that enabled your success as a state champion?

What piece of advice would you give to a head coach who wants to win a state championship?

What do you consider the one most important aspect of your championship team this year? How did you develop that in your program?

We are fortunate to have had a history that includes some significant success; I believe that fed our players to want to become a part of the tradition that had been established. How did you develop that in your program? "Tradition never graduates."

Virginia AAA

Coach: Richard Morgan

School: Oscar Smith High School

City: Chesapeake

2011 Record: 14-1, 9-0

Championship Game Results:

Oscar Smith	47
Centreville (Clifton)	21

State Championships at School: 2

Years as Head Coach: 10

Years at Current School: 10

State Championships Won as Head Coach: 2

What did you do differently this year from the other programs in your league, your section, your state that enabled your success as a state champion?

What piece of advice would you give to a head coach who wants to win a state championship?

What do you consider the one most important aspect of your championship team this year? How did you develop that in your program?

"Greatness is uncommon; therefore, it will not be achieved by the common man" is the motto we lived by in 2011. We had to get everyone in the program to strive for greatness in what they do every day. As coaches, we refused to let them settle for just getting by. We didn't let them just blend in. Every player was held accountable to stand out and make a difference. They were not allowed to be common. Day by day, we got better and better—until we got to a point where we couldn't be beaten.

Virginia VISFA Division 4

Coach: Mike Henderson

School: Blessed Sacrament Huguenot High School

City: Powhatan

2011 Record: 9-2, 3-1

Championship Game Results:

    Blessed Sacrament-Huguenot   18
    Greenbriar Christian (Chesapeake) 14

State Championships at School: 5

Years as Head Coach: 15

Years at Current School: 15

State Championships Won as Head Coach: 5

What did you do differently this year from the other programs in your league, your section, your state that enabled your success as a state champion?

We break practice down into four quarters and try to win each quarter. I give a score at the end of each quarter to let them know how I feel we are practicing. Also, we condition at the end of each quarter instead of all at the end.

What piece of advice would you give to a head coach who wants to win a state championship?

Starting in ninth grade, really get to know your kids. Make sure they understand you care about them personally; get to know what they like away from the field. Once they know you care, they will do anything for you.

What do you consider the one most important aspect of your championship team this year? How did you develop that in your program?

Chemistry. See previous answer.

Virginia VISFA 2

Coach: Ed Homer

School: Christchurch School

City: Christchurch

2011 Record: 10-0, 4-0

Championship Game Results:

Christchurch	48
Potomac (McLean)	15

State Championships at School: 1

Years as Head Coach: 25

Years at Current School: 20

State Championships Won as Head Coach: 1

What did you do differently this year from the other programs in your league, your section, your state that enabled your success as a state champion?

Each year, you hope to get the most from each player and, in turn, give them the best possible experience. Requiring selflessness in practice is difficult given the volume of expectations on their time. Football must be important to all the players all the time, but they are still kids. It comes down to a critical mass of leaders, and those leaders usually have to be seniors. If your senior class is not focused on success (demanding full effort and attention from the team as much as possible all season long), you will have difficulty with team climate. This year, we had a significant number of leaders in the senior class, so that when one or two players had bad days, they did not take the whole team with them. The general climate of all practices was both positive and productive. The juniors did not challenge the leadership of seniors. If they tried, they stuck out as outliers. The seniors on my team were in control; we had three captains and tried to focus on them being punctual and focused, and then demanding the same from their teammates.

What piece of advice would you give to a head coach who wants to win a state championship?

Be patient. Unless you have a way to constantly stock the shelves with great players and great leaders, you get your chance every once in a while to have the stars align, and then you have to get to work. If you have a good crew returning, start now (winter). Strongly encourage them all to participate in another sport. Specializing is not as beneficial as it may seem. They need to compete, period. This year, we had a strong group of seniors, several of whom played for us as freshmen. They had seen their share of being the underdog, and had already faced an uphill battle on the field. It was their time, and they knew it. Remain very positive when this arrives, and tell them how good they are. Focus on this all the time. "We will not be successful if …" should be replaced with "We will be successful if …" Although this is necessary all the time, it is especially necessary when you have a legitimate shot at being successful week in and week out. If you have been patient with your kids, now is the time for them to reap the benefits of their patience and hard work.

What do you consider the one most important aspect of your championship team this year? How did you develop that in your program?

Experience, strength, ownership.

Experience: Kids who had played in lots of varsity games come into their senior year with great confidence. This is hard; real experience means they had to pay their dues. If you have a large team (numbers) and have played only juniors and seniors, my experience does not fit. We are small, and thus this year was the culmination of three (or in a couple of cases, four) years of hard work and preparation.

Strength: Weight training for physical strength is a must, but so is competing—for overall strength. Our most valuable players were all multiple-sport athletes. The one or two kids that did not really start for other teams (in all cases, they were kids that had injuries and were thus not able to play a winter or spring sport last year) were valuable cogs in the wheel, but the true strength (spiritual, physical, mental) came from the kids that had competed in varsity sports for three (or four) years in more than one sport. As I mentioned earlier, patience was the key for us.

Ownership: I do not call the offense or the defense, but I make sure that I am responsible for the kids knowing the assignments at each position. Each coach has a position responsibility on each side of the ball. All off-field preparation is, in the end, my responsibility. When the coaches call plays, we have to know that the kids can execute them. We all share that ownership/responsibility. I think my assistant coaches know they are valuable, and I do not usurp their authority on the game field. If I need to step in and make a call, I try to make sure that it is before a call is made and not overturning a call by a coordinator (we have a staff of four).

Virginia Division 2

Coach: Kevin Saunders
School: Gretna High School

City: Gretna

2011 Record: 13-2, 5-1

Championship Game Results:

Gretna	21
Goochland	16

State Championships at School: 5

Years as Head Coach: 18

Years at Current School: 3

State Championships Won as Head Coach: 1

What did you do differently this year from the other programs in your league, your section, your state that enabled your success as a state champion?

What piece of advice would you give to a head coach who wants to win a state championship?

What do you consider the one most important aspect of your championship team this year? How did you develop that in your program?

Our school is an incredible story of success. At one point before I arrived, Gretna had lost 44 consecutive games and now have won five of the past nine state championships. I took over in 2010 after Gretna had won back-to-back states. We have won these state championships with three different head coaches. When I took over, I had a reputation of taking over terrible programs and turning them into winners, so when I took this job, people expected us to be rebuilding, but all we have done in my three years is play in two state championships, winning one. Our football program currently holds the state's longest streak of winning 10 or more games for nine consecutive years.

- The first key for me with our kids is that we are a spread team. I was a wing-T guy until I showed up, but I am not stupid. They weren't broke, so no need to fix it. So we stayed in the spread, and rest is history.
- I am a defensive guy, so the biggest key was us changing what we did on defense. I changed them from a 3 stack to a 40 with four linebackers sometimes only two, so more of a 4-2. This year, we never gave up more than two touchdowns in any game, and even in the blowouts our second team was tremendous.

The number-one thing we do is quit running (conditioning) after the third game after Mondays. We still do a cardio run on Mondays, which is a light day for us. I truly believe that our kids must play fast. So we practice fast, train (weights) fast, and coach fast. We don't not stop practice to correct a player; we (coaches) take him out, put his back-up in, and he gets coached then while he is not in the drill. We spend a lot of time on technique and assignments.

I really believe the players must have fresh legs and be in a great frame of mind.

West Virginia Division A

Coach: Mike Young

School: Central Catholic High School

City: Wheeling

2011 Record: 13-1

Championship Game Results:

Central Catholic	35
Williamstown	21

State Championships at School: 9

Years as Head Coach: 16

Years at Current School: 7

State Championships Won as Head Coach: 5

What did you do differently this year from the other programs in your league, your section, your state that enabled your success as a state champion?

What piece of advice would you give to a head coach who wants to win a state championship?

What do you consider the one most important aspect of your championship team this year? How did you develop that in your program?

Our goal from the beginning was to improve every day, working on something to be better than the day before. Our goal was to defend the state title and to play December 3 in the championship game—a goal we reached together.

Wisconsin Division 2

Coach: Pat Rice

School: Waunakee High School

City: Waunakee

2011 Record: 14-0, 6-0

Championship Game Results:

Waunakee	45
Waterford	0

State Championships at School: 5

Years as Head Coach: 20

Years at Current School: 20

State Championships Won as Head Coach: 5

What did you do differently this year from the other programs in your league, your section, your state that enabled your success as a state champion?

I'm not sure we do anything completely unique. We try to do what we do. We believe in being fundamentally sound in all three phases of the game. I think we do an outstanding job in preparation week-to-week as well as year-round. Then, taking it from the whiteboards and film room on to the field. I think we run an extremely efficient practice; it is very uptempo with a tremendous number of reps. We believe that our attention to detail during the week and our number of reps allow our players to understand the game plan and play fast.

What piece of advice would you give to a head coach who wants to win a state championship?

There are no shortcuts. There is not a magic bullet that cures everything. You just need to grind—in-season and off-season—in so many different areas, all of which are key to the success of your program. We try never to be satisfied and take things for granted; we are always looking to improve and get better. The other thought may sound cliché, but worrying about the game in front of you. We really try to stay in the moment and understand what we need to do that week to be successful. We believe that if we have a great week in terms of preparation, this will show on Friday nights.

What do you consider the one most important aspect of your championship team this year? How did you develop that in your program?

Our team-first mentality was really our key this season—the idea that everyone has roles, and no matter what your specific role is, it is critical to the team and to the success of the team. This really led to tremendous team chemistry and leadership. We were all in from the student assistants to the players to the staff. It is very hard to articulate, but when that happens, you become a very difficult team for your opponents to deal with.

Wyoming Six-Man

Coach: Michael Bates

School: Little Snake River Valley High School

City: Baggs

2011 Record: 11-0, 4-0

Championship Game Results:

    Little Snake River   54
    Dubois   33

State Championships at School: 2

Years as Head Coach: 5

Years at Current School: 3

State Championships Won as Head Coach: 2

What did you do differently this year from the other programs in your league, your section, your state that enabled your success as a state champion?

What piece of advice would you give to a head coach who wants to win a state championship?

What do you consider the one most important aspect of your championship team this year? How did you develop that in your program?

I really did not change what I did from previous years. The advice I would give to other coaches is that the season does not begin in August; it really begins after the last season ends. Now, some kids do other sports, and that is okay. As a matter of fact, I push for that. However, if they are not in a sport, I try to get them in a weight room and/or to study film. The connections are what I feel to be the strongest part of our program. Kids have buy-in, which goes a long way. I develop connections by having team-bonding times besides the weight room or field. I get them to understand that the season is won out of season, not during. If you want to win a state championship, this is what it takes. I also let the kids know that schedules are irrelevant; playing in November is not. That is what we want, to be playing then when over 75 percent of the teams are not dressing. The biggest advice that I could give another coach is: make connections with the kids; make them understand that you value each and every one of the players.

Wyoming 4A

Coach: Don Julian

School: Sheridan High School

City: Sheridan

2011 Record: 11-1, 8-1

Championship Game Results:

    Sheridan   42
    East (Cheyenne)   14

State Championships at School: 23

Years as Head Coach: 14

Years at Current School: 5

State Championships Won as Head Coach: 6

What did you do differently this year from the other programs in your league, your section, your state that enabled your success as a state championship?

We hold a leadership camp in the mountains with our seniors prior to the start of the season. At this camp, we set goals, discuss issues like drugs and alcohol, do problem-solving activities, and help our seniors understand the type of leadership we need to be champions. We feel like it is a great component of our success, and we don't even have a football in camp.

What piece of advice would you give to a head coach who wants to win a state championship?

The one piece of advice I'd give to a head coach wanting to win a state championship is: "As your seniors go, your season goes." Your best players must be your best workers and must be servants within your program.

What do you consider the one most important aspect of your championship team this year? How did you develop that in your program?

We had an incredible sense of unity, leadership, and confidence within our program this year. It can be attributed to the group of seniors we had leading and their willingness to listen to their coaches, and the group of underclassmen who were willing to follow.

About the Author

Chris Fore is a veteran high school football coach and athletic director from Southern California. His education includes a master's degree in coaching and athletic administration from Concordia University, and a bachelor's degree in biblical studies. Fore has earned the Certified Athletic Administrator distinction from the National Interscholastic Athletic Administrators Association.

Fore started his coaching career while still a senior in high school at Fallbrook High School in Southern California. A tragic car accident ended his playing career, but started his coaching career. In 2003, at 27 years of age, Fore took over as the head coach at Linfield Christian in Temecula, California. While at Linfield Christian, the Lions reached the CIF Semi Finals in 2002 and 2004; in the 30 years prior to that, they had only made it this far twice. Capistrano Valley Christian School of San Juan Capistrano, California recruited him to turn their program around. In his first year there, the Eagles improved to a 5-5 record after being winless the year before he started. In 2010, his team won the league championship, and his peers voted Fore as the Coach of the Year. The Eagles won six league championships under his direction, a school record. He became the athletic director and varsity special teams coordinator at Excelsior Charter School in Victorville, California in May 2012. That same year, Excelsior won the CIF Championship in eight-man football and finished the season as MaxPreps highest ranked eight-man team in California.

Fore also runs COACHFORE.ORG, a popular coaching blog among coaches nationwide. He also works as a consultant for football programs and schools nationwide—he specializes in the hiring process and organizational management. His consulting business can be found at www.eightlaces.org.

He has been married to Christine since 2004; they have three beautiful children: Nate, Taylor, and Josiah.